Is There a Heaven for a "G"?

Is There a Heaven for a "G"?

A Pastoral Care Approach to Gang Violence

DANIELLE J. BUHURO

Foreword by JoAnne Marie Terrell
Introduction by Sharon Ellis Davis

RESOURCE *Publications* · Eugene, Oregon

IS THERE A HEAVEN FOR A "G"?
A Pastoral Care Approach to Gang Violence

Resource Publications
An Imprint of Wipf and Stock Publishers
199 W. 8th Ave., Suite 3
Eugene, OR 97401

www.wipfandstock.com

PAPERBACK ISBN: 978-1-5326-0851-3
HARDCOVER ISBN: 978-1-5326-0853-7
EBOOK ISBN: 978-1-5326-0852-0

Manufactured in the U.S.A.   JANUARY 12, 2017

To my maternal grandmother,
who now rests with the ancestors,
Agnes Haymon.

She inspired me to always write
because writing unleashes the soul.

Contents

Foreword

THE WORLD HEALTH ORGANIZATION defines interpersonal violence as "the intentional use of physical force or power, threatened or actual, against another person, that either results in or has a high likelihood of resulting in injury, death, psychological harm, maldevelopment or deprivation."[1] It may include abuse, bullying, dating (or relationship) violence, sexual violence, youth violence, and gang violence.[2] In all its forms, interpersonal violence has profound psychological, social, and spiritual effects on individuals, families, and neighborhoods, as well as on the larger communities in which neighborhoods are situated. Unquestionably, the problem of interpersonal violence has serious consequences for institutions within communities, including schools and, especially, religious organizations, for it begs of the synagogue, the temple, the mosque, and the church the question of how each faith's scripture, beliefs, and practices propose to remedy the tragedy and disruption interpersonal violence wreaks in so many lives. Christian scripture asserts that such violence has its seed in unchecked thoughts that find harbor in all of our (all-too-human) hearts, "for out of the heart come evil thoughts, murder, adultery, sexual

---

1. Dahlberg and Krug, "Violence: A Global Public Health Problem," in *World Report on Violence and Health*, edited by Krug et al. (Geneva: WHO, 2002), 1–21.

2. "Interpersonal Violence," http://us.reachout.com/facts/factsheet/interpersonal-violence.

immorality, theft, false testimony, slander" (Matt 15:19) against each other as individuals and, most infelicitously, as the collective body of Christ. Violence is unneighborliness, and like cancer cells in a vital organ, its affected cells replicate, break away from their point of origin, and metastasize, manifesting in other vulnerable sites in the body. Indeed, interpersonal violence is a public health crisis, a virus of pandemic proportions.

I picked up the manuscript for *Is There a Heaven for a "G"?* with the thought in mind that it would be an academic—if pastoral—treatment of gang violence and perhaps other associated forms of interpersonal violence. The author, Danielle Buhuro, is a Christian chaplain working the trauma unit in a hospital situated in a major metropolitan area, Chicago, Illinois, the epicenter of a recent uptick in murders[3] in spite of a downward trend in violent crime across the United States.[4] The book is instead a poignant memoir of Buhuro's priestly, prophetic, and noble efforts to provide pastoral care among, with, and for those embroiled in the complex web of gang violence. Buhuro shares the insight she has gained from her interaction with victims felled by violence and those who survived it. Her fresh approach challenges ministers, chaplaincy corps, and medical staff who are shocked by the ways of the world and wearied by caregiving, to rehumanize our connections to surviving victims of gang violence by understanding the contexts of risk they have to negotiate for identity, status, and belonging. In her role as prophet and priest, Buhuro challenges family members of felled victims and survivors, survivors and our friends, to see ourselves as *human beings* and, therefore, as having a moral imperative to know and relate to the *Divine Reality* within ourselves and others. For it is in the joy of being human— realizing our purpose, coming to know and refining our desires,

3. Park and Patterson, "Chicago: The Shocking Numbers behind the Violence," CNN.com, August 30, 2016, http://www.cnn.com/2016/08/29/us/chicago-violence-shootings.

4. Ehrenfreund, "We've Had a Massive Decline in Gun Violence in the United States. Here's Why," *Washington Post*, December 3, 2015, https://www.washingtonpost.com/news/wonk/wp/2015/12/03/weve-had-a-massive-decline-in-gun-violence-in-the-united-states-heres-why.

gifts, callings, and relationships, and actualizing all of this—that we experience inchoately what the hymnodist Frances J. Crosby describes as "a foretaste of glory divine,"[5] what theologians call the eschaton, and what lay Christians, and countless folks from other faiths, imagine as heaven.

Even though (perhaps, *because*) I have taught a course on AIDS and Violence at Chicago Theological Seminary for more than twenty years, I had not anticipated that *Is There a Heaven for a "G"?* would trigger the trauma of the interpersonal violence I experienced over my lifetime. Reading the manuscript took me back to the life-changing event of my mother's murder in 1973. Not to the shocking, tear-filled, and seemingly unreal, immediate aftermath of her death, but to the caregivers who accompanied me as a child struggling to understand the emotional storm I was enduring. These included police officers who came to let my elder sister and me know what had happened, one of whom allowed me to cry in his arms (I still remember the strong smell of his leather jacket); my grandfather, whose very presence was certainty that things would be alright, eventually; and my aunt and uncle, who became my guardians, who bore patiently with me, taught me to make myself useful in the church, and put me on a path to becoming. I am genuinely grateful for the comfort and love I received in those woeful days of my violently interrupted youth.

I never received, though, the *blessed assurance* that there was a heaven for my mother, neither from my grandfather, who was a pastor, teacher, and planter of churches, nor from my uncle and late aunt, a pastor and missionary. The sad thing is, I do not think I asked, because, though I was a child, I knew intuitively that the prevailing evangelical theology could not concede that much grace to my mother, who was presumed a sinner because when she died, she was addicted, unchurched, and "living in sin," that is, with a man to whom she was not married, the same man who took her life. Even though I could not name these then, I privately resented the theological implications of the church's capacity to withhold the "assurance of pardon" from those who need it the most

---

5. "Blessed Assurance," lyrics by Fanny Crosby (hymn, 1873).

because of their private anguish and their inability to get or remain on a path of becoming, for whatever reasons, and to reserve it for those who say they are "saved" but continue to abuse the privileges of a relationship with Christ. This simplistic moral theory fails to take into account the psychological, social, economic, and political context of struggle, gender oppression, sexual repression, and racial interdiction in which my black mother tried to navigate her life but was ravaged instead by intra- and interpersonal violence.

Forty years later, for African Americans, the context of struggle remains largely unchanged. *Is There a Heaven for a "G"?* does an admirable job of situating the historical context out of which gang violence emerged as an attempt on the part of disenfranchised folks to create agency in their lives. The author also critiques the church and the role of evangelical religion in the buttressing of our violent context through its limited hermeneutics, vigorous promotion of pietistic faith and the idea of individual responsibility for sin, and its practice of condemning perpetrators, felled victims, and surviving victims of violence, without a concomitant condemnation of the violent society that produces them. In that sense, the book seeks to remedy and not perpetuate the violent theologies that have not only wreaked havoc in people's lives, but also left the church in the unenviable position of losing ground in the fight to "win souls"[6] because it has ignored the reality and context in which those same souls—the addicted, the unchurched, those "living in sin," and those embroiled in interpersonal violence—are engaged.

The Reverend JoAnne Marie Terrell, PhD, LHD
Chicago Theological Seminary

---

6. Cf. Tickle, *The Great Emergence: How Christianity Is Changing and Why* (Grand Rapids: Baker, 2012).

From Domestic Violence to Gang Violence

Making the Connections

IN THIS INTRODUCTION, I was asked to reflect on the question "Is there a connection between domestic violence and gang violence?" My answer to this question is an unequivocal, "Yes!" This introduction seeks to give a larger response to a simple "Yes"! My personal and professional experiences, having served as a police officer (31 years), pastor (25 years) and public theologian/ethicist (10 years), a professor (26 years), a pastoral care provider (20 years), and a parent (for over 45 years), are derived from a plethora of contexts of which I have attempted to locate meaning as they inform my ministry. Making meaning is a lifelong and necessary task to enable society to develop effective strategies and tools for intervention, prevention and healing.

Domestic Violence, also known as Intimate Partner Violence (IPV), has, as its root cause, the need to assert power and control over another person. This violence can manifest itself as physical, emotional, financial, or sexual. Yet, in each circumstance, power and control is the major impetus. In my twenty-five-plus years as a pastoral care giver and pastor I have provided pastoral care to victim/survivors of domestic violence. Many/most of the victims/survivors were women who were experiencing abuse from their spouse/partner or their children. And, I realized early on in these relationships the ways the abuse experienced within the family structure could easily impact relationships within the larger community especially as it relates to the impact on children. In the same light, I have ministered with and provided care for children and youth who did not have the needed support of their parents and there were major disruptions and chaos within their family system that usually involved drugs and/or alcohol. And, as an ethicist I have witnessed the structural violence imposed through policies, laws and other systemic issues of power, control, and privilege which has facilitated, furthered, and as some posit, caused, tremendous disruption and instability within the family system that has led to additional stress and violence within families.

Many of the families I have encountered are urban, middle to low income, as well as poor and single-parent households, and this introduction represents this population. The violence within the family structure as well as through structural/systemic violence put upon families, have had a significant impact on family systems and, I believe, is a major catalyst to violence within families as well as in society. Yet, the system, rather than seeking ways to assist these families toward stabilization, tends to demonize, blame, stereotype, shame, and criminalize victims and perpetrators of crime. As a result, we tend to spend more time blaming violence on poor/negligent parenting styles, absences of fathers within the household, etc., rather than conducting a systemic analysis of how families got there in the first place. This is to never neglect how we all have to be accountable for our actions. Yet, to lay total blame on individuals or group of individuals represents an inadequate response leading to inadequate solutions to end violence. Thus, the cycle continues. Violence spills out of the household into other institutions and into the street. Youth begin to search for places where they can belong, feel safe, and be heard. When that place is not in the home, deviant behavior can develop and the impact can be devastating. Gang violence is one of those manifestations. Consequently, I choose to also include structural/systemic issues, which disempowers and is oppressive toward families, as domestic violence. It is impossible to speak about one (Intimate Partner

Violence), without being inclusive of systemic issues of oppression within families in the population I have served over the years. The following stories represent the many families I have ministered with throughout my career and demonstrates the connection of domestic violence to gang violence.

As a pastoral care giver, I have heard story after story of women who were victim/survivors of domestic violence and subsequently separated or divorced their abusive partner. Yet, the story of the abuse is only the tip of the iceberg of how the abuse had impacted the entire family. One survivor struggled with her teenage boy who was, now, also emotional and sometimes physically abusive to the mother. This story is not atypical of many survivors of domestic violence. The children are also victims of domestic violence by virtue of their presence within the household and sometimes directly experience the physical abuse. These children may also experience issues of anger from the absence of the father in the home and in their lives. The acting out at home always seemed to lead to acting out within the school system or in social settings. One mother realized her son could not hold a female relationship because he would ultimately disrespect the girl through neglect, indifference, and/or emotional abuse. The main question of this mother, and in other cases was, "Is there something I have done wrong as a parent to cause my child to act in this way?" As a pastoral care provider I attempt to affirm her as a parent, assure her she should not take on total blame, while at the same time, helping her to understand her basic role as a parent to her obviously wounded child. Yet, as previously mentioned, many parents are left with feelings of guilt and shame and are disempowered through their inability to be a change agent within their family structure. What eventually happens to the children?

As a pastor of a new church start located in the far suburbs of Chicago, I was shocked to see so many children come to the church without their parents. I grew up in an environment where parents took their children to church or at least assigned someone to take us or care for us once we were there. However, these children came without their parents Sunday after Sunday. We never experienced meeting many of the parents. A couple of parents eventually joined the church community. Yet, there were a great number of children (below 13) who attended worship without even an inquisitive visit from a parent to at least see what we were doing within the four walls of the church and if their child was in a safe environment. We eventually discovered that many of the parents were experiencing drug and alcohol abuse. This and other issues of employment, multiple families living together, and a sense of apathy, prohibited our ability to develop a relationship with many of the parent(s). And, when we were able, there was not a real concern for connecting with the environment to support their children. Many of the children preferred coming to the church to going home. We had one child visit our church. The child was very young (5–6 years old). We assumed the child was with the other children. However, after the children left the child remained in the church. The child was too young to tell us where he lived. We drove around the neighborhood looking for someone who could identify him. Eventually someone did. We discovered, the child lived almost a mile away from the house. When we rang the doorbell, the mother answered the door. There were several children in the house. And, at a glimpse, the house looked to be in disarray. She took the child from us, said thanks, and shut the door. That was the last we saw of this young boy. Our church community is known for gang violence and hearing gun shots was the norm. On many occasions we noticed young boys running around the neighborhood acting in ways we described as practicing being a gang member. Perhaps with the neglect in the household, they believed this was their only hope. Perhaps the church was the only option, other than the streets, for them. If this pattern of disruption and neglect within the family system continues, what happens to the children?

As a professor, I taught a course titled "Mass Incarceration and the Criminal Justice System." This class involved contextual experiences to go along with the theory learned within the classroom setting. The class spent the day in the juvenile court system and one day was spent at a local transitional house for ex-offenders. In this setting we met with a young man who volunteered to share his life experiences before entering the criminal justice system. He, as in many stories we heard that day, spoke about his life as a child and how he lived in poverty. As a young child, he would look outside the doors of his house and see the desolation (broken glass, abandoned apartments, etc.). He realized early on that his life should not be one of poverty. He realized something was disarrayed in the ways he was forced to live. Living this kind of life led him into negative criminal activities that eventually led him into jail. This young man took full accountability for his actions and did not blame the system or anyone else for his actions. Yet, he realized and asserted, "I knew that I should not have been living in this kind of poverty." This is but one example of systemic oppression where we are forced to ask, "Why are families living in poverty, in a world of plenty? Why are parents not earning a living wage? Why are families forced to live in substandard housing? Why is punishment, criminalization, and imprisonment the reward for children raised in this environment who were looking for a way out?" When we examine the connection between domestic violence and gang violence we have to also engage in a critical analysis of the systems who acted as the initial agents of abuse within families. When families experience disempowerment and other forms of oppression, how does this impact criminal activity? What happens to the children?

As a police officer, I had the opportunity to hire high school children and young adults to work in the department under the mayor's summer program. One of my duties was to serve as their supervisor along with conducting criminal background checks to ensure they had no record. I hired many children with a questionable background because I believed it was imperative to give these youth a fair and safe start in the employment sector while also providing mentoring and care, if only for a few months. I remember having to arrest one of the male young adults who, during the program, had stolen an automobile. With tears in my eyes, I walked him to the lock up. With tears in his eyes he handed me his house keys and asked me to please get them to his girlfriend whom he lived with. I don't remember his name. I don't remember his address. And, I don't remember his story. I do remember that many of the children came from low income families. And, some of the children I picked up personally and drove them to work. Who is investing in our children? Who is giving them second chances and opportunities? The criminal justice system's focus on punishment inflicts further harm on families. Sending youth and young adults to jail with no rehabilitation plan only furthers disruption in families and provides them with more negative learned behavior from other persons who are incarcerated.

What am I saying? To understand what I am saying, it is important to understand what I am not saying. I am not attempting to explain what goes on in families as *the* cause for youth and adults joining gangs or engaging in any criminal activities. I am well aware that there are many families who experience some of the same issues and the family turns out to be wonderful, smart, and productive members of society. I wish I could predict factors that could conclusively state when a child will become involved gang activity. However, what I am saying is there is a connection to gang violence when there is major disruption within a family system which can be attributed to the various interlocking systems of power and control outside as well as inside the family unit. I am asserting that the basic family system is foundational to developing a healthy society. And, I am asserting that if we want to end gang violence we have to focus majorly on the family system. And these systems have function. What I posit is "Yes" there is a connection. And, the connection is, all of these families are families "*in risk.*"

The term "in-risk" was coined by a gentleman named Darnell Jones, a staff member of a violence prevention/intervention program known as Cease Fire. Jones coined this term in 2014. The term "At-Risk" makes the assumption that factors are present that may impact an individual or family one day. I appropriate the term "In-Risk", however to acknowledge that consequences are already in play. And, key to understanding the connection between domestic violence and gang violence is understanding the oppressive structures, internal to a household, makes the entire family high risk, and even more vulnerable to outside influences such as gangs and other criminal activity.

How do we address these multiple needs, professionally known as *intersectionality*? One way is to find ways to address the intersections of one's family life and how they give rise to other negative behaviors, rather than focus mainly on the deviant behavior and punishment. Dr. Danielle Buhuro, in her book *Is There a Heaven for a "G?,"* seeks to provide pastoral care techniques and tools that have as its framework a social and contextual connection. She does not look for a "one-size-fit-all" approach to care and situates ones experience as a viable starting place to develop strategic intervention and care models. "Is there a heaven for a G?" is a quintessential question we, especially those of the faith community, must all answer. Life has been hell for many gang members long before gang members began raising hell! Can we, as caregivers, help them to find a piece of heaven here on earth through our advocacy, care/counseling, and the prophetic presence we offer in our professional ministry settings? As I was completing this introduction I overheard on the news the police superintendent of Chicago being interviewed regarding the violence in Chicago. Once again, a gang member had just shot a man and critically injured him, making him Chicago's five hundredth shooting victim this year. The man was shot on the lawn of his home. The police superintendent made the following statement about the violence, and I will end my introduction with his words:

> You show me a man without hope and I will show you a man who is willing to pick up a gun and do anything.
>
> **EDDIE JOHNSON, ABC NEWS, SEPTEMBER 7, 2016**

Rev. Sharon Ellis Davis, MDiv, PhD
Affiliate Professor, McCormick Theological Seminary

who is in charge?
Adult in Custody or Inme-

How many brothas fell victim to tha streetz
Rest in peace young nigga,
there's a Heaven for a "G"
be a lie, if I told ya that I never thought of death
my niggas, we tha last ones left
but life goes on. . . . [1]

TUPAC SHAKUR

1. "Life Goes On," lyrics at http://www.azlyrics.com/lyrics/2pac/lifegoes on.html.

Jumah Boycott

All Hell's about to Break Loose

The Moment when the Pager Goes Off

It's 9:45 P.M. I am sitting in the Emergency Room's on-call chaplain office with the door closed, resting comfortably in a Lazy Boy reclining chair and wondering what I am going to wear in the morning for Sunday worship. Fortunately, the small on-call office is located right inside the emergency department, next door to the quiet room, giving the chaplain instant access at the drop of a dime to anything that jumps off in the ED. Unfortunately, this means I have to hear all the alarms, bells, signals, overhead pages, shouting doctors, overworked nurses, cries from sick patients, screaming babies who don't want to get their shots and, of course, staff who can easily knock on my office door at any given. . . .

BEEP! BEEP! BEEP!

Suddenly, the on-call pager sounds. Oh my God! I hate the sound of that pager. I usually jump out of my skin at the sound. Which usually upsets my stomach and causes pee to come from out of nowhere. I quickly grab the pager from the desk and read the text message: 17-year-old male, gunshot wound to the abdomen and thighs multiple times. "Here we go again," I think to myself as I adjust my clothes and head out the door.

They really don't pay me enough for this. Thank God I'm not married and don't have any kids. We'd be broker than I already am.

1

And don't give me anything about this is training and it'll pay off in the end. Blah. Blah. Blah. Don't tell me how after this year I'm gonna have four units of CPE (clinical pastoral education) and I can go anywhere in the world and land a full-time chaplain gig making $50,000. More blah. . . . That doesn't have anything to do with me right now.

On my way to the trauma bay in the ER, I quickly head to the bathroom first. Make sure I wash my hands. Adjust my hair. Fix my clothes. Nobody wants a sloppy chaplain coming to minister to them. People judge outside appearances first. I grin at the bathroom mirror to check my teeth. Nothing like having food stuck in your teeth to really embarrass you. I check my pockets for a peppermint. Stinky breath can be the worst. Can't offend anybody with stinky breath. Check my nose. Wanna make sure there's no booger in there. Look at my eyes. Wanna make sure there's no crud in there. I give myself another look up and down. Do I look professional enough? Is my outfit too casual? I'm only a chaplain resident so I can't afford to look nice like some of the staff chaplains.

Suddenly, the pager goes off again. "What now?" I think to myself. I pull out my portable phone trying to juggle the pager and my anxiety.

"Hi this is the chaplain."

"Chaplain, we've got a fetal demise up here. Mom's doing horrible. We need you now!"

The nurse's voice is frantic. She sounds like she's being held hostage in a bank at gunpoint.

"I'm in the Emergency Room for a code yellow. Please give me a minute nurse."

"No, this woman is a basket case. We need you now!"

I hear a woman screaming in the background.

"That's my baby! No! No! No! Y'all killed my baby!"

"Nurse, I'll be there shortly."

"Yeah, hurry up!"

I'm still in the ER, waiting at the ambulance entrance to see about the gunshot victim. I'm almost out of breath running like a bat out of hell from the bathroom to the trauma bay. I didn't want to miss anything. Stuff happens fast around here. You blink and you might miss a lot. I feel like I'm about to have a heart attack. I think to myself, "So much for prepping myself in the bathroom." I look like I've been running a marathon by now.

I check my pockets for pen and paper to write names down. Oh damn. I forgot a pen on my desk. I turn around and run back to the on-call office quickly. I wonder if family has been notified. As I quickly walk back to the on-call room I start thinking about what I'm gonna say. Hmmmm. What to say? What to say? There's no manual for this you know. I hate that. When I first started in this residency I tried to look for a book about this: "How to provide pastoral care to a person coming into the hospital as a result of gang violence?" Unfortunately, nothing came back in my Google search. Go figure. They got pastoral care books on EVERYTHING but that. Cancer has a book. AIDS/HIV has a book. Chronic illness has a book. Hell, even domestic violence has a book, but not gang violence! Which is hard considering all the people who are in gangs today. As of 2012, approximately 850,000 persons were reported gang members in roughly 30,000 gangs, according to the Office of Juvenile Justice and Delinquency Prevention (OJJDP).[1] I'd be happy if somebody came out with a damn book. Grabbed my pen from the office and headed back to the emergency room.

My pager goes off again. I've just made it back to the ambulance entrance in the ER. I lean up against the wall in the hallway, all the while peering out the two automatic glass doors for any sign of the paramedics. I pull out my portable phone to return the page. Nurses are prepping one of the nearby trauma bay rooms. They started laughing and giggling about a patient in another room who looks like George Clooney.

"Hi, this is the chaplain."

"Yes, this is public safety. We have family here in the ER waiting room to see that 17-year-old who just got here."

"I wanna see my son right fucking now!"

I hear a man yell in the background.

---

1. Egley et al., "Highlights of the 2012 National Youth Gang Survey," 1.

"Sir, I have the chaplain on the phone now and she'll be here in a moment—"

"Chaplain? I don't wanna see no damn chaplain!"

I interrupt the gentleman I hear screaming in the background. "Wait officer, he's not here yet. We're still waiting for the paramedics."

Click. The officer hangs up immediately.

Beep! Beep! Beep!

I'm really beginning to hate this damn pager. I read the alpha text message:

"Patient in ICU wants to sign a power of attorney now!"

I turn to the charge nurse who's shuffling papers and putting away charts at the nurses station.

"How long before the Code Yellow Trauma gets here?"

"Uhhhh, I think you got about 10 minutes. They're stuck in traffic."

I never understand how the hell the paramedics get stuck in traffic but without any hesitation I quickly race up to the ICU to complete the power of attorney. Fifteen minutes later I'm headed back down to the ER.

Beep! Beep! Beep! I check the pager again. "This family in the ER is going crazy now chaplain, I need some help ASAP!"

I arrived right at the ER main entrance when I figured I better not go through the front door where I'd then come face to face with this anxious family. I walk instead to another side entrance that's farther away for "employees only." Thank God I wore my comfortable flats and resisted the urge to be cute today. I walk around the twenty-seven-bed ER until I find a cloud of medical staff huddled in one of the trauma bay rooms. I find a doctor breathing heavy as he's taking off his gloves and face mask. Sweat is coming down the sides of his face.

"Let's call it! Time of death?"

"10:00 p.m.," a nurse responds.

My heart drops.

"Wait, doc, try some more!" I dive into the room, pushing past all the medical staff.

"Please, doc, do the CPR longer!"

"Sorry, he's gone." The doctor pulls out a clipboard and starts writing.

I become enraged.

"How long did you do chest compressions, doc?! He just got here!"

Tears began to fill my eyes.

"We did everything, chaplain. Trust me."

The doctor looks around at the nursing staff.

"Now, somebody start cleaning this room up, please."

He looks back around in my direction.

"Let me know when you're ready to talk to family, I've got some other patients to check on."

"I'm ready now, doc, to go talk to the—"

He hurriedly whisks away into another room. I look at an African American boy's lifeless body lying on the bed. Blood is everywhere. One side of his stomach has sunken in. Apparently that's where one of the bullets hit him. Nurses and certified nursing assistants (CNAs) start packing up medical equipment. A couple of radiology techs roll a big machine out of the room. I grab a pair of gloves and start picking up pieces of the boy's clothes from off the floor.

"Here's a bag."

A nurse hands me a plastic bag.

"That's evidence now. Police are on their way."

We begin stuffing all his belongings in the bag and cleaning up the room, careful not to touch his body and disrupt the medical examiners investigation. My mind starts to wander again. I can't possibly land a full-time chaplain gig. Besides it's seven or eight seminaries and theological institutions in this city alone. Which means each of those seminaries graduate at least fifteen people with the Master of Divinity degree (the formal education requirement to land a full-time staff chaplain gig) so I got strict competition for landing a gig anyway. Ugggghhhh.

Beep! Beep! Beep!

The pager goes off again. Damn! What a night! I read the message: "21-year-old female gunshot wound to the abdomen." I quickly race to the quiet room, making sure the lights are turned on, the room is clean and there's a couple of boxes of tissue along with enough chairs.

Beep! Beep! Beep!

The pager goes off again. What the fuck! The message reads: "When is someone gonna come talk to this family of the 17-year-old? Family's growing restless!"

I look at my watch and notice it's 10:45 p.m. I've done more in the past hour than some people do during their entire shift. I head to the ER waiting room. I immediately flip my badge to the backside so family won't see my title. The title "chaplain" always freaks people out at first.

I notice a large African American family has gathered. I look at a public safety officer who's standing nearby. He points to the family. Mind you, he didn't point discreetly. Some family members notice him pointing at them and now me walking toward them. They quickly look me up and down. I walk over to a gentleman who looks the most visibly distraught.

"Sir, my name is Danielle and I work with the hospital."

"Yeah who are you?"

Other family start to gather around us.

"I work with the hospital, sir. Please come with me."

The family looks hesitant. I try to be as calm as possible so as not to make a scene and upset other visitors and sick patients in the waiting room waiting to be seen.

"Please come with me."

This time I'm a little more stern. They slowly start to follow me. We walk past a woman who's vomited on the floor. I motion to public safety to call environmental services. Another woman grabs my arm.

"Ma'am, I've been waiting for over an hour now. Are you the manager?"

I look behind me to see how close the family is following me. They are a few feet away.

I start whispering.

"No ma'am, I'm the chaplain, but I can—"

The woman quickly looks at the distraught family following me then turns back toward me.

"Ohhhhhh that's ok."

She puts two and two together and then she totally makes my night a living hell. She turns toward the sobbing father as he catches up to me.

"I'm soooo sorry for your loss."

He quickly peers in my direction.

"What!?"

"Sir, please come with me!" I quickly grab the gentleman's arm and usher him through another door to our quiet room.

The family follows us and walks into the quiet room. All eyes are on me.

"I'm going to go get the doctor to speak with you."

The father looks at me as tears roll down his cheek.

"Hey Ms. Lady, how's my son?"

A knot forms in my stomach. I hate this part of the job.

"I'm going to go get the doctor to come and speak with you."

I try to say this as kind and soft as possible. A woman grabs my wrist. Her nose is running.

"How's my nephew, ma'am?"

I grab one of the boxes of tissue sitting on a table in the quiet room and hand her a few pieces. Tissue is used all the time in this profession. I've killed many trees over the years.

"I really can't say, ma'am. I'm going to get the doctor and have him speak with you."

I hate lying. I hate lying. I hate lying. But, chaplains here aren't allowed to tell family when patients have died. Only doctors can do that. I look around the room. It must be about fifteen people crowded in this small room. Some are sitting on each other's lap. Others don't wanna sit so they are leaning against a wall. A couple are sitting on the phone texting. I hate cell phones in this line of work. People send a text then next thing you know a thousand people are in that waiting room. A little old lady rises from a couch. She reminds me of my grandmother. Tears start welling up in my eyes. She walks over to me and grabs my hand.

"Baby, you don't have to keep nothing from us. Just tell us about my grandson. His momma died three months ago and he ain't been right since. . . . Hey, we ain't been right since."

Tears fall down my eyes. The aunt hands me back one of her tissues.

"I'm sorry to hear about his mom. What happened?"

"Cancer snuck up on her, honey."

"Oh my gosh."

"Yeah." She looks back at the sobbing father. "My 'son-in-love' had to go out and get another job to support my grandson and his two younger brothers."

"Hmmm . . ."

I nod my head empathically and rub the grandmothers hand.

"My grandson thought he'd help his daddy out with bills by going out and trying to make some money with these hoodlums. But I told him that's not what we are about in this family. His mother was a principal of a high school on the north side and his dad is an electrician."

The father began to weep again as other family began to console him.

"We good Christian folk and we didn't raise Abel to be like this, ma'am."

"I understand, ma'am. It's not your fault. Would you like some water?"

They nod yes.

"I'm going to get the doctor and bring you back some water."

They nod thank you. I watch the grandmother turn and waddle back to the couch.

I race back into the ER and look for the doctor. I find him leaning against the wall with his arms crossed at the ambulance entrance. He looks so tired. He almost didn't notice me.

"Another gang member . . ." He says this sarcastically.

"Who?"

"We got a 21-year-old female who was suppose to be here already, but the paramedics got stopped by a train."

I hate the fact that a train route is nearby the hospital because many times paramedics get stopped by freight trains passing by and critical patients die.

"How's she doing, doc?"

"Paramedics say she's not gonna make it."

"That sucks. . . . Hey doc, can you please come talk to the family of the 17-year-old? They're in the quiet room now."

He seems to stare off into space for a minute.

"Give me a minute chaplain, I'm busy. . . ."

I wait patiently for one minute. He continues to stare off into space.

"Ok, you ready now, doc?"

"Ok, let's go." He doesn't move. "You ready, chaplain?"

"Yes, sir, I'm ready." He still doesn't move. I reach out to grab his hand. Tears fall down his eyes.

"I'm so sick of this shit."

I understand. This hospital is a Level I trauma center which takes in at least one GSW (gunshot wound) victim every afternoon and evening, Sunday through Saturday. Gun violence doesn't take a break. The warmer months are worse. The warmer the weather the more GSWs will occur. We see a rise especially during the summer months.

Some doctors feel deeply for their patients. But other doctors can grow a little insensitive. The redundancy makes them emotionally paralyzed at times. I don't blame them. I'd probably feel the same way. Another doctor walks past us.

"Get it together, Jeff, that's what they do. They kill each other. They're animals."

I become livid and peer intently at this other doctor.

"He's still a human being, doc," I respond. He rolls his eyes, "I know."

That's the hard part of my job in all this. Having to challenge the doctors. Having to hold the doctors and nurses and medical staff accountable to be sensitive. We do this as chaplains. We walk a fine line between being a part of the interdisciplinary team and, at the same time, advocating for the patients. I'm also embarrassed at times. Most of the patients who come into the hospital as a result of gang violence are African American or Latino American. While most of the doctors and other medical staff are European American or Indian American. I'm black and it's during moments like these that my black pride always rises up. I don't know if the doctors are being racist or, like I said earlier, they're just emotionally paralyzed from seeing it so much. Maybe it's a little of both. What frustrates me is the myths around gangs. Sometimes, the white staff think it's mainly black and Hispanic young boys in gangs. However, many whites and Asian Americans are in gangs too.[2] Unfortunately, most of them don't come to this particular hospital though so medical staff don't get to SEE them. Perception is shaped by what people see.

I look at the first doctor. "You ready to go talk to this family now?"

"Yeah, let's go."

We walk together to the quiet room in silence. I open the door and walk in first with the doctor behind me. I hold the door open for him. As the doctor walks in, I look out into the emergency room waiting area which is still packed with sick people and visitors. I catch the eye of the public safety officer. He begins walking to me and I motion for him to stay back. Sometimes our public safety officers can trigger African American families because of the history of police brutality toward African Americans. The father stands up to greet the doctor. As I allow the door to slowly close, the public safety officer continues to make his way to me in the quiet room. He catches the door before it closes.

"Chaplain, can I see you for a minute?"

I look pissed that he's pulling me out of the room as the doctor's getting ready to deliver the bad news. I step out of the room into the hallway and let the door close behind me.

"What do you want? You know I'm kinda busy right—"

2. National Institute of Justice, "What Is a Gang? Definitions," http://www.nij.gov/topics/crime/gangs/pages/definitions.aspx.

"AAAAAAHHHHHHHHHHHHHH!!!" BOOM!

I hear a loud scream from inside the quiet room. The officer looks at me in the hallway.

"Did you forget about the fetal demise in labor and delivery? It's nuts up there!"

Suddenly the door to the quiet room swings open and the doctor hollers out.

"Code Blue!"

I peer inside the room and see the grandmother lying motionless on the floor!

FUCK!

Anxiety in Pastoral Care

The moment the hospital on-call pager rings, a chaplain resident pushes through their own anxiety to provide pastoral care. Sometimes, that anxiety is as a result of other extenuating factors, such as the frustration of receiving a small stipend for their work. In gang violence work, the chaplain resident may even struggle with what to say to patients and families given the lack of resources on this topic as of yet. Also, chaplain residents finds themselves managing the anxiety of the medical staff, highlighting how chaplain ministry also encompasses not only providing a pastoral presence to patients and families, but medical staff as well.

Managing anxiety is very important in pastoral care ministry. First, it's important to discuss the origins of anxiety. British psychologist John Bowlby highlights how anxiety develops in human beings during childhood.[3] Bowlby's findings developed his theory of abandonment, which summarizes how infants experience a threatening moment when they are physically separated from their mother. "This perception of threat leads to the production of various hormones that stimulate the infant physically and emotionally."[4] These hormones are anxiety producing.

---

3. Richardson, *Creating a Healthier Church*, 44.
4. Ibid.

There are many "threats" I've experienced in providing pastoral care. When I reflected on these threats, I discovered something more sinister, more earth shattering. After much reflection, I came face to face with my own sense of vulnerability. I'm threatened by the unknown in pastoral care ministry. I'm threatened by not knowing what I'm walking into when the hospital pager rings. I'm threatened by not knowing what the pastoral care request will be when I pick up the phone to return a page. I'm threatened by not knowing what to say when I arrive to greet a family. I'm threatened by not knowing what to say to a family when I'm waiting for a doctor to come into a room and deliver bad news. I'm threatened by not knowing how the family will react to news that their loved one has died. The doctor leaves the room after delivering the bad news, but I'm threatened to stay in this space and minister to this family. I'm threatened in journeying with this family who are now open, exposed, naked and vulnerable in these grieving moments. I'm threatened by being open and vulnerable myself, siting in the space of a family's pain and not being able to do anything about it. If I could, I would trade my own life for the life of their loved one. But I can't. More than anything, I'm threatened by my own pastoral confidence. Am I really fit to do this job?

What I've learned is how to manage my own anxiety during these tragic pastoral care encounters. First, I practice reciting positive affirmations to myself when my anxiety rises. I recite positive affirmations that affirm my call to ministry and affirm my pastoral competency. Second, I become aware of what's going on within my body physically. I listen to my heart rate. Gage my pulse. I take a moment to drink some ounces of water, stretch, and practice a few simple yoga positions. Last but not least, I meditate, asking my Holy and Divine One to give me strength and calm my anxiety.

More than anything I've learned that my own sense of anxiety will spread like wildfire if I'm not careful. Reflecting on family systems theory in the parish ministry context, Ronald Richardson highlights how anxiety experienced by one person, in particular the pastor, has the potential to impact the larger congregation. The chaplain is the pastor in the hospital context while the hospital staff serves as the congregation. I learned that my own anxiety as chaplain impacts hospital staff and also patients and families that I serve. I wonder how many patients and families I have unfortunately transmitted my anxiety to.

An underlying theme in pastoral care is one's ability to manage multiple incidents at the same time. Chaplain residents learn quickly how to assess and triage various incidents that arise at the drop of a dime. In an ideal world, it would be nice if incidents occurred one by one in a linear fashion, but this is not the case. Chaplain residents learn the necessity of juggling effortlessly. In this juggle, I've learned the importance of managing my anxiety so that I don't bleed on patients, families and hospital staff, especially in light of the new cases of gang violence that arrive at the front door of hospital emergency rooms almost every day.

Is There a Heaven for a "G"?

Gang violence has begun a vicious cycle that permeates the fabric of our society. This book is entitled *Is There a Heaven for a "G"?* in the hopes that someplace, somewhere, someone becomes encouraged to put down a gun, or their intent to use a gun, and picks up a deeper sense of spirituality that beckons a renewed calling to live life with mission and purpose. This is not an evangelical text that judges our brothers and sisters who have created meaningful lives and lifestyles as a part of gangs, but rather this is a piece of work that reminds the religious right, the fundamentally conservative, that even gang members have the right to experience heaven, a place filled with grace and mercy. A heaven that none of us own or control and thus have no right to determine who gets to go to and/or who doesn't. Usually, our Christian community tells people that in order to experience "our" heaven, gang members must leave their gangs and abandon their violent lifestyles. However, this is not that type of book. While one hope is that gang members decrease violence, this selection is not intended to ask people to disconnect from their gang affiliations. One can be part of a gang, social group, fraternity, sorority, or clique and not participate in violence. However, this book is intended to remind persons that no matter where they are on life's journey they too can experience heaven, even if they are still actively a "G" or "gangster." This is a selection filled with love and not condemnation, grace and not guilt, liberation and not shame.

This book is written to inform chaplains, pastors, ministers and other clergy how to provide pastoral care to gang members. While there are Christian references made in this selection, it can be an educational piece for non-Christians as well. The education provided in this selection is not Christology-centered but rather humanity-centered. This is also a reflective memoir that highlights how and what this writer has learned from her encounters with gang members while a chaplain resident at a Level I trauma center in a southern suburb outside of Chicago. Thus, readers are asked to reflect too. Each chapter provides a reflective moment for this writer to discuss important thought-provoking and "aha" moments. At the end of each chapter are also "Food for Thought" reflective questions for the reader to reflect on individually or in a group. While the context of this selection is based mainly in a hospital and the writer speaks from the perspective of a chaplain, the information given can be used by anyone in any environment where one interacts with gang members.

This book, *Is There a Heaven for A "G"?*, highlights important dynamics in providing pastoral care to gang members and summarizes a pastoral care approach that focuses on empathy, education and empowerment. In the first chapter, "In Between a Rock and a Hard Place: Talking to the Family," readers learn how chaplains initiate conversations with family members who come to the hospital as a result of a loved one's involvement in gang violence. These initial conversations can be difficult at times, leaning on a chaplain's ability to finely weave words together in a fabric of nonjudgmental and supportive presence. This chapters speaks to the fears of the family, the communication style of the chaplain and of most importance, the method by which the chaplain builds trust with families. Chapter 2, "A Dream Deferred: The Moment When the Patient Dies," outlines what can be a surprising and

Annotation

painful grief process when a patient unfortunately dies as a result of gang violence. Families come face to face with the reality that death of a loved one means death of someone with dreams, aspirations and hope, someone who could have been the glue of the family, someone who could have been the family's "superman" or "superwoman" whom the family depended on for various reasons. Also, this chapter explains how families make burial arrangements as well as interact with the police department and county medical examiner's office.

Chapter 3, "Connection Is Key," begins the meat of this book, in which I outline a methodology for providing pastoral care to surviving gang member patients. The first step in gaining connection with gang members is learning and understanding how certain factors contribute to gang membership and lead to gang violence. First, I discuss racism and socioeconomic factors. Next, I highlight how the period of African enslavement in US history impacts African American gang membership and violence. I then suggest our current culture of violence is also very influential, followed by our ill-perceptions of how we even define what constitutes a "gang." Next, this chapter speaks about empathy or "connectedness," highlighting steps chaplains and clergy can initiate to foster relationships with gang members, including story-listening, which will later lead to breakthrough, hopefully. Chapter 4 is the center of the meat of this sandwich: "Holding Accountability and Educating Gang Member Patients." In this chapter, readers learn the importance of how to employ accountability, constructive confrontation and nonjudgmental challenge to gang member patients, tackling such questions as "How do we help gang members self-differentiate a new identity apart from their gang family?" Chapter 5, "Ending on Empowerment," reminds readers of the importance of ending a pastoral care visit on a high note or positive side. In the words of my grandmother, "Don't undress me without helping me put my clothes back on." This chapter is an attempt to help gang member patients put their clothes back on, covering their nakedness and vulnerabilities before the pastoral encounter ends.

Last but not least, I understand that providing pastoral care can be a very grueling task. Thus, chaplains and clergy persons would do well to engage in healthy self-care strategies to release the physical, emotional and spiritual drain of working in traumatic encounters with gang members. This is the focus of chapter 6, "What about Me? Self-Care for the Pastoral Care Provider to Practice." Finally, chapter 7, "Where Do We Go from Here?," provides some concluding self-reflecting thoughts on next steps in this line of work.

I hope this book provides readers with education and grace to give to someone else who needs to hear this message for healing, hope and wholeness. There is so much miseducation and myths about gangs and gang violence permeating our society. Please don't internalize and spread the stereotypes. Hopefully, you, as reader, are transformed just as much if not more than your audience. Enjoy the journey!

Chapter 1

In Between a Rock and a Hard Place

Talking to the Family

"I'm so sorry for your loss."

I know I'm not suppose to say this, but I can't think of anything at the moment. My head is spinning. Sorry means sympathy. But people don't need sympathy. During times of loss, people need empathy. Sympathy means sorry, but empathy means connection. Hallmark makes tons of money selling cards that are inaccurately phrased, "Sorry for your loss."

"I can't believe they killed my baby!"

The mother clutched the deceased body of her thirty-one-week-old baby. He was beautiful. He looked so perfect. Perfect ten fingers. Perfect ten toes. Perfect two ears. Perfect two eyes. Perfect one nose. Curly brown hair. Cute fat cheeks. Adorable little lips. He looked just perfect. But he had a not-so-perfect heart. He looked like he was sleeping. His lifeless body reminded me of the gunshot wound victim in the emergency room.

"Why do you believe the hospital killed your baby?"

"Cuz I was fine when I came in here!"

She begins to cry in anguish. Her husband rises from the couch. He's wearing a cool shirt, reading "I'm a proud papa!" His legs are shaking. He looks like he's about to fall any minute now.

17

He places his arm around his wife. They peer at the baby in her arms. Melancholy sets in. Then silence.

KNOCK! KNOCK! KNOCK!

An older woman peeps her head in the room.

"Carmen . . ."

Both mom and dad look up toward the door. The mother yells out a painful scream. My heart sinks. The daughter starts yelling to the top of her lungs.

"Mama! Mataron a mi bebe!"

The older woman gently opens the door and slowly walks over to the bed. She's rubbing her hands. Her hands are trembling. She's got a balled up piece of worn tissue in one hand. Tears roll down her eyes. She's bright red. She begins quietly whispering something to herself.

"Ave Maria llena eres de gracia el Senor es contigo . . ."

I'm regretting the fact that I never paid attention in my high school and college Spanish class. She makes her way to the bed and I figure out that this must be the patient's mother and the deceased baby's grandmother. I step to the side so the grandmother can move closer to her daughter. She grabs her daughter's long curly hair and begins lovingly stroking the solemn mom's forehead. The husband looks at his mother-in-law with disappointment and failure written all over his face.

"Soy mama lo siento."

The mother walks to the other side of the bed to embrace the husband. She cups his face in her small frail hands and softly kisses one side of his stoic face.

"It's ok son, you tried your best."

Grandma looks at me.

"Who are you?"

I'm shocked that she speaks both Spanish and English.

"My name is Danielle and I'm a chaplain. I came by to provide your daughter and son-in-law with support during this time."

"Awe. Thank you."

The grandmother looks at the door. She motions for me to please step outside with her. She looks at her daughter and son-in-law.

"Tenemos que tener el bebé bautizado y bendecido por un sacerdote. Voy a hablar con ella llamando al Padre Michael. Voy a estar en un minuto."

I wish I knew what she just said. The grandmother grabs my hand and pulls me outside. She smiles at her daughter and gently pulls the door shut. Even though she is frail, she seems so strong. So in control. So matter of fact. Once the door is closed she turns to look at me then . . . BAM! She collapses to the floor, covering her face with her hands. Nurses nearby run over to us. I can't take it! Not another person passing out on me! A nurse grabs some medical equipment from a drawer nearby.

"Ma'am are you ok?"

I jump in, "She's ok, just grieving."

The grandmother sits up and lays against the hospital room door. Her eyes are bloodshot red now. The nurses turn to walk away. One nurse looks empathetically at the grandmother.

"I'll bring you some more tissue and water."

"Gracias."

The grandmother turns her attention to me. She starts whispering.

"They've been trying for years now to have a baby. She's my only daughter and—"

BEEP! BEEP! BEEP!

I quickly silence my pager with one hand, not looking at it so I can be fully present and not distract the grandmother.

"Do you have to go?"

"It's ok I can stay for a few more minutes. What were you saying about your daughter?"

"Well I'm 76 years old and she's my only daughter. Most of my brothers and sisters have died and went on to be with the Lord now. I've got only one sister left. She's got a 21-year-old but she's so irresponsible we don't know when she's gonna settle down. My daughter is our only hope but she has . . . problems!"

The grandmother drops her head and starts to cry again. I wrap my arms around her.

"What type of problems does she have?"

The grandmother begins moaning and groaning.

"She's no good at making babies!"

I kneel down to sit on the floor next to the grandmother. Didn't know my job would require this. Glad I'm not wearing any fancy clothes.

"My heart goes out to you and your family. I can't imagine how you must be feeling. How can we support you during this time?"

"I'm never gonna be a grandma! Our family line is gonna die!"

"I have some resources I can provide you and your daughter with ma–"

BEEP! BEEP! BEEP!

I feel bad having to leave the grandmother in this condition but I've ignored this page once and I can't do it again. Hopefully, no one's called my vice president and reported me after the first unanswered page. I look at the grandmother.

"I'll be right back ma'am. I have to return this page."

I rise from the floor.

"Take your time, baby, I'm not going anywhere."

She remains seated on the floor.

She pulls out a rosary from around her neck. I walk toward the nurses station to return the page. Unfortunately my portable phone battery is dead now. My phone battery can't hang like I can, like I must.

"Hi this is Danielle, the chaplain."

"Yeah Chap, this is public safety, family has finally arrived for that other GSW."

"I'm on my way."

Ugggghhhhh I forgot about that. I walk back over to the grandmother of the miscarriage that's sitting on the floor with her back leaned against the hospital room door. I bend down to talk to the grandmother.

"I can call our on-call priest to baptize and bless your grand baby."

"That would be great but the baby's already . . . you know."

"I understand, we have some priests who are sensitive and still give—"

BEEP! BEEP! BEEP!

"I'm sorry I must go now."

I hurriedly pull a piece of paper from my notebook. I'm jittery now.

"There's a wonderful group called Fertility for Colored Girls that can help."

I scribble their number and website on the paper.

"Their number is 773-273-9870 and the website is www.fertilityforcoloredgirls.org."

I almost throw the paper at her and take off running down the hall. She barely catches the paper and jumps to her feet.

"THANK YOU, YOUNG LADY!"

I yell down the hall, "De nada!"

That's the only thing I remember from my Spanish classes. I hop on an elevator to make it to the ER, trying to straighten my clothes when the doors close and wipe dust from my pants after sitting on the floor. And I still need to go to the intensive care unit to check on the other GSW's family. The grandmother collapsed in the quiet room when she got the news that her grandson died. She was rushed to the ICU. The family all wandered like a herd of sheep to the ICU. I couldn't imagine how they must've been feeling. Two serious events at the same time in one family! Whheeew! I look at my watch. It's 12 midnight on the dot.

"Wait, where the hell is my relief?"

The next chaplain was suppose to be here at 11:00 p.m. I was suppose to leave thirty minutes ago. I totally lost track of time with all that's going on. Maybe he called in. I'll check my office voice mail messages lat—

BEEP! BEEP! BEEP! As I'm walking back to the ER I stopped in a hallway to use a phone mounted on a wall.

"Good evening this is the chaplain may I he—"

"Yes, Rev, the patient in telemetry room 666 is requesting a Bible."

I resist the temptation to laugh about the room number.

"Ok no problem, I'm heading to a trauma in the ER so can he give me about 30 minutes?"

"No, chaplain, he says he needs it now. He says he's hearing screams in his room. Just come now!"

CLICK!

She hangs up on me. I'm always surprised when patients find God in the middle of the night when they come to the hospital. If you're that close to God then you should bring your own Bible with you to the hospital dammit! I quickly deliver the Bible then head to the ER. When I arrive back to the ER I can't find the family. I assume it's a large family because the patient is Hispanic. Usually African American and Hispanic families have large families. I run to the public safety officer standing by the ER waiting room.

BEEP! BEEP! BEEP!

"I'm here! I'm here!" I'm half out of breath but I'm here.

"Where have you been I've been paging you like crazy???!!!"

I ignore his questions.

"Where's the family?"

"I put her in the waiting room for you already Rev."

"Wait who? What do you mean?"

"It's only one person from the family here. An old lady. She looks like she's in her 60s, 70s or something. She must be the grandmother. Tell her to call her son or daughter so they can come see about their kid. They probably out partying and smoking dope or something."

I frown up.

"No judgments tonight, Officer. Thank you!"

"Hmmmm. Yeah ok."

"Ok."

I walk away and head to the quiet room. Why would a grandmother make it to the hospital before a mom or dad? I walk into the quiet room. The lights are dim. It looks a little bad from the previous family. Cups of water are everywhere. Used tissue balls are on the couch and table. There's no more tissue in the tissue box which is laying upside down on the floor. Damn this place looks like Pearl Harbor! I didn't have time to clean the room in between families.

"Good evening, my name is Danielle and I'm the chaplain."

"Hi."

I gently reach out and hold her hands in mine.

"I'm sorry you had to come here in the middle of the night."

There I go with that damn "sorry" again. I keep forgetting.

"It's ok, I'm used to it. My car just drives here on it's own now. I probably should set up a room here as many times as Carmen has me here."

We both smile lightly.

"I'm going to have the doctor come speak to you now. Before I go can I get you anything?"

"How's she doing?"

"I don't know, ma'am. Let me have the doctor come speak to you. Can I get you anything?"

She looks disappointed.

"No." She goes to sit back down on one of the couches that looks the most clean out of the entire room.

"Is there anyone I can call to be with you so that you're not alone?" She slowly shakes her head from left to right.

"No, I've been trying to reach my sister but her phone keeps going to voicemail so I called my pastor and he's on his way."

"Ok, I'll be right back."

BEEP! BEEP! BEEP!

I walk over to the ER public safety officer and standing next to him I notice a tall African American gentleman in a pinstriped suit wearing a clerical collar.

"Yes officer?"

"Hi chaplain, this is Apostle Joseph Harding from New Faith. He's here to see the older woman in the quiet room."

I'm immediately turned off. This "apostle" is wearing a burgundy Sunday suit at one o'clock in the morning. He's got on sunglasses too. REALLY! Is there any sun on the inside of this hospital? And a huge gold cross around his neck. I can see every feature of Jesus' face on that cross!

"Hi Apostle, come with me."

"I must say I'm surprised to see a woman chaplain here tonight."

BOOM!

And now I know I definitely don't like him. We begin walking to the quiet room. I feel the stares of visitors. We can't be incognito with his flashy attire. I'm almost a little embarrassed.

"Why are you surprised?"

"I was expecting a white male Catholic priest or something..."

"I understand. Times have changed now, Apostle." I murmur under my breath, "Catch up."

We arrive to the room and I slowly open the door.

"I see they've even hired a cute chaplain too..."

I pretend like I didn't hear him. He can't even respect boundaries. Go figure.

"Ma'am here's you pastor."

She rises to greet him. He holds her in his arms for a moment. She begins to cry all over again. She raises both hands in the air. Her face scrunched up.

"Why Pastor???!!! Why???!!!!"

He starts rubbing her back.

"Shhhhh. Don't talk like that. We don't ask why. Remember you have to trust God!" And now I know I'm about to throw up! This is why I hate church pastors in my line of work. The woman takes a deep breath. She lets go of his hug and sits back down on the couch. The pastor looks around the room and turns his nose up. He's afraid to sit down. He remains standing and turns his attention back to his parishioner.

"Remember, God promised to never give you more than you can handle. So stop crying. You have to be strong. Your faith depends on it."

I can't take it anymore. I interrupt him before he can commit more illegitimate theological murdering. I get down on one knee and hug the woman.

"It's ok if you want to cry. You are human. This is hard. You don't have to hold it in. If you want to cry, go for it. If you want to yell, go for it. If you want to scream, go for it. God understands. This doesn't mean you don't have any faith."

I peer at the pastor and roll my eyes. He looks dumbfounded. I rise from the floor.

"Let me get the doctor."

The pastor notices my attitude and he catches one too.

"And bring back a broom and dustpan to clean this nasty room will ya?"

I pretend I didn't hear him again, making sure the door quickly closes behind me. As I walk out I look at the woman again and I notice she looks oddly familiar. I find the doctor and grab him before he can go into another person's room.

"Hey doc, family for the 21-year-old Hispanic GSW is here. How's she doing?"

"She was dead by the time she got here. Those damn train tracks killed her. Paramedics did everything they could. Nothing helped."

My heart sank. Two deaths in four hours all because of guns in the wrong hands.

We walked into the quiet room together. I tried to play poker face and not give anything away. The woman musters enough energy to rise to her feet. The doctor starts talking first.

"How are you related, ma'am?"

"I'm her mother."

My mouth drops open. So does the doctor's. He quickly gathers himself.

"Uhhhmmm oh ok. . . ."

The woman gives him a little grace.

"I know I get that look a lot. I had Carmen late in life when I was in my mid-forties."

A soft smile tries to reveal itself through all her pain. The doctor tries to recover and continue talking. He lowers his voice and looks at the floor. He closes his eyes.

"Unfortunately, Carmen did not make it."

Silence. Tears well up in the pastor's eyes. I look at the mother. "What did you say?"

The doctor gulps.

"Unfortunately, Carmen passed away."

Silence again. The mother never takes her eyes off the doctor. The silence kills the doctor so he starts talking a bunch of medical terminology mumbo jumbo about exactly how she died. The mother looks confused. I intercede again.

"So basically doctor one of the bullets hit a main artery?"

The doctor looks at me startled.

"Well, yes. Thank you, chaplain."

I've discovered that there's so much that goes into talking with a family during events like this. First, I have to find the doctor and prep him or her, calming any anxiety they feel. Then I have to walk the family to that God awful quiet room and hope that they don't catch a clue about why I'm really bringing them there. Then I have to manage huge families that turn the hospital into a free-for-all gathering space by calling up every possible person they know and inviting them to the hospital to see the patient. Then I have to do what I'm doing now and translate for the doctors when they start talking all this medical mumbo jumbo to the families. The mother continues to look lifeless and peer at the doctor. She hasn't moved or changed her eye stare. Silence again. The doctor turns and heads to the door.

"If you have any other questions, feel free to let the chaplain know and she can come get me."

No response. The doctor abruptly leaves. I think his own nervousness got to him. I look at the pastor. He stares silently at the walls. I look back at the mother. She stares at the door that the doctor just walked out of.

"I hated that she joined that gang. . . ."

Her voice trails off. I feel a deep sense of uselessness. My mind begins to wonder about my young cousin who was killed one evening while he was out joyriding with friends. I try to remain focused on the present case at hand. I turn to the mother and hope she doesn't notice my eyes, which are beginning to water. I grab a sheet of paper from my small chaplain's notepad. I pass the paper and a pen to the mother.

"If you could write your daughter a letter in these moments what would you say?"

The woman begins to jot down some words. She pauses in between words to wipe her face. Every now and then tears escape her cheeks and fall on the paper. I wish I could take her pain away. But I feel helpless.

RING! RING! RING!

The mother pulls out her cell phone. She looks at the display then cracks a small smile.

"One moment, this is my sister finally!"

She begins talking in Spanish to her sister on the other end of the line. I immediately pray that the sister can handle the unfortunate news that's about to be a bombshell dropped on her. Suddenly, the mother begins crying all over again. I hear screams coming from the telephone. Then the mother drops the phone.

"I can't talk to her chaplain, can you give her directions to us?"

Her pastor begins to console her again.

"Sure no problem." I bend over to pick up the phone from the floor. The distance from standing upright to leaning down to the floor seems like a Grand Canyon.

"Hi, I'm the chaplain."

"Yes, I'm trying to get to the Emergency Room?"

"Are you here already?"

"Yes I am."

I'm a bit puzzled. I thought she was at home or something. Her voice sounds familiar.

I give her directions on finding the ER's entrance, then I hang up the phone.

"Your sister's on the way."

I look at the mother. She rises to her feet. Still a bit shaken. The pastor stands too. The mother turns to him and motions for him to sit back down. He obeys accordingly. I wonder where his big mouth has disappeared to. The mother focuses her attention toward me.

"Can you walk me to the main entrance?"

"Sure no problem."

She wraps her arm in mine. We walk quietly to the main entrance. The mother stops walking for a moment and motions to a nearby restroom sign.

"I gotta go, hold on a minute."

She limps away. An elevator is nearby. It's computer operated voice announces:

"You've arrived at the ER entrance."

The elevator doors slowly open. I quite naturally look to see who's inside. The doors open and out walks the grandmother of the fetal demise I encountered in the labor and delivery unit.

"Ma'am, can I help you? The exit is not this way, but I can show you the—"

As she walks off the elevator, the grandmother looks through me as if she's seen a ghost. She suddenly stops and looks in the direction of the restrooms. I turn my focus to the restrooms and notice the mother limping out. The grandmother at the elevator squints her eyes.

"Is that my sister?"

Both women's eyes connect. Then the unthinkable happens. The grandmother screams.

"No! No! No! My niece Carmen isn't dead, is she?"

DAMN! DAMN! DAMN! I think to myself. Tonight's gonna be a long night.

When There Really Are No Right Words to Say: A Chaplain's Own Vulnerability in Pastoral Care

I wish I had the right words to say. I hate feeling speechless. I hate looking dumb. I hate feeling dumb. Usually, when I arrive at these spaces and places in my life, I can cover. I've learned to cover well. Unfortunately, chaplaincy has a profound way of reminding one of their own shortcomings, flaws and hang ups. And guess what? They are front and center in chaplaincy for the world to see. There is one pivotal dynamic that my shortcomings and flaws remind me of. A dynamic, a word I'd rather never let escape my mouth. Vulnerability. An interesting word isn't it? In the pastoral care encounter I am open and exposed. Naked perhaps. The patients see me just as much as I see them. That's the scariness of this ministry. I believe that's why this ministry is not for the faint of heart. This ministry causes you to ignore your Superman side and come face to face with your Clark Kent side. If this wasn't enough something more grueling occurs.

Our ministry to patients in the hospital is one that reminds us of our not-so-favorable experiences. That patient in the hospital bed is not just simply a patient. Nope! That patient turns into your mother, your father, your grandmother. That patient turns into an experience that happened to you in elementary school, that incident involving your high school bully, your first kiss, your first driving permit, your graduation. What happens in the hospital room triggers all of your unsettled life events. Those issues and concerns that you have not fully grieved and healed from. The pain and anguish that visits you every time these frustrating experiences sneak back into your consciousness. It's important to reject inappropriate transference or projection for the patient's sake, nonetheless.

Last but not least, chaplaincy reminds me that I don't have all the answers. Pastoral care is an art, not a science. In mathematical science, one plus one always equals two. Two plus two always equals four and likewise, four plus four always equals eight. Pastoral care is not this definitive. The "answer" could be anything. The answer is not confined, it's limitless. What people need may be something that's not in my purview. An answer that I don't own or control.

Ironically, what if I told you that most people already know the answers to their questions. Most people already know what resolutions or comforts they need during times of tragedy, crisis and chaos. What people need however is a listening ear to vent and share. That listening ear could be a physical ear of a loved one who created safe space or a sheet of paper, a journal that gives one space to let their true authentic feelings be heard without judgment.

What makes this job even more cumbersome is the task of remaining present in the midst of someone's pain. During sad, mad and scared times I want to run out the room as fast as I can. But I can't. I've been called to watch tears fall down faces. Hear screams and shouts of "Why?" Listen to wrestling of theological questions of suffering. See grief. See despair. See hopelessness. I don't think the average person could do it. So then it would seem as if the hospital chaplain is a bit crazy for wanting to be in this line of work. Well, here's to the crazy ones. The social misfits. The outcasts. The square pegs trying to get through round holes. Here's to all the people that just ain't right. These people actually make us ponder. These people force us to act. These people change the world!

Building Trust

Building trust in the chaplain-patient-family relationship is pivotal in pastoral care work. There are several steps a chaplain can take to build trust. Oftentimes, trust is built even before the family or patient meets the chaplain. When I arrive to work at the beginning of my shift, I walk to and check out the emergency room's quiet room. Most hospitals have quiet rooms in various locations of their hospital. There's a quiet room in the emergency room, intensive care unit, and on each general/medical floor. A quiet room is a small room that can usually seat three to ten people comfortably. It houses one or two couches, chairs and/or desks. It's adorned with beautiful pictures, and soft lighting. It may even have a television and/or vending machine. The quiet room is a separate space for grieving families to have to themselves that allows them to cry, scream, yell or even holler without disturbing other patients and families in the clinical unit. The quiet room allows a grieving family to gather privately with other family and friends without other patients, staff and visitors inappropriately spectating or gazing at them. I refer to this as "grief tourism."

The quiet room is also a space where medical staff can have confidential conversations with family about the health condition of their loved ones. It provides a space where doctors can ask sensitive questions about the patient's condition that may serve as a resource for how to best care for a patient. If the reason that led to a patient being hospitalized requires a criminal investigation, such as a homicide, motor vehicle accident/collision or traumatic fall, the quiet room also serves as a confidential, sensitive space where local or state police can interview relatives.

When I start my work shift, I visit the key quiet rooms I may need such as the emergency room and ICU ones, and survey them for cleanliness and safety concerns. There's nothing worse than bringing a family into a quiet room and noticing that there's leftover used tissue or half-drank cups of water in the room from the family of a previous patient encounter. Also, I survey the room to make sure there is nothing broken, such as pictures, lamps, chairs, etc., destroyed by the previous family. During times of grief, sometimes families punch holes in the wall or knock over and break lamps that I need to report to our environmental services and/or building and grounds department.

Building trust also entails providing families with ample tissue and water while they are utilizing the quiet room space along with caring for families' basic human needs. I always check in with such questions as "When was the last time you ate something?" or "Is their anyone I can call for you to be with you so you're not alone during this time?" Doing this, I believe, is demonstrating hospitality. I also check in with family about what I consider are important personal matters or triaging life needs: "Do you need me to call your job and let them know you won't make it to work today?"; "Who's responsible for picking up your children from school today?"; "If you are feeling light-headed in these moments, do you have your blood pressure medicine?"; "Do you have asthma and if so, do you have your inhaler with you?"; "Do you need me to have a nurse or doctor see you for any of your health challenges?"

Trust is also built through nonjudgment and open body language. At some hospitals, it is the responsibility of the chaplain to call the family and inform them that their loved one has been involved in a traumatic crisis. This has to be done with as much skill and grace as possible. If the patient has died, chaplains are never to deliver this information. This information can only be delivered by a doctor. So, chaplains walk a fine line. Also, chaplains never want to arouse families too much then ask them to get behind a wheel and drive to the hospital, which may lead to families becoming involved in car accidents or having heart attacks behind the wheel due to their own anxiety. Oftentimes chaplains don't announce that they are chaplains over the phone because most people believe that when a chaplain calls or visits that means someone has died. I may say something such as, "Hi, my name is Danielle and I'm a staff worker at _____ Hospital. I just wanted to inform you that your loved one _____ has come into our hospital for medical treatment and we would like for you to come see him/her now." I have both a calmness and urgency in my voice. If family don't arrive in thirty to forty-five minutes, I make the phone call again.

When family arrive I demonstrate a nonjudgmental presence. I refrain from using language that is racist, sexist, classist or homophobic. I refrain from making any political statements. I make sure my language is free from sexual/erotic connotations. I also maintain an open, welcoming posture. I refrain from crossing my arms, give direct eye contact, cup my hands and double check that my feet are positioned in an open stance.

Last but not least, building trust means acting as a liaison between the medical staff and families. For example, I remind doctors that family have been waiting in the quiet room for quite some time. I provide pastoral care to the doctor's own sense of anxiety to bring them into the quiet room quickly so as not to keep the family waiting in suspense for an extended amount of time about the condition of their loved one.

When the Church Pastor Says All the Wrong Things

Church pastors sometimes have a tendency to say all the wrong things. In my line of work, we sometimes despise church pastors. They have difficulty sitting in places of pain and being quiet. Most church pastors need to fill the space with empty clichés and inappropriate Bible passages. Yes, God can put more on you than you can bear. No, I don't have to trust God in season and out of season. No, my faith is not dependent on whether or not I cry in these moments of anguish or question God.

When we discuss the topic of gang violence, we need church pastors to provide tangible results not empty theology and meaningless verbiage. We need church pastors to provide gang violence safe havens in their churches. Do you offer a social service outreach program in your church that redirects neighborhood youth from participating in acts of violence? We need church pastors to work with their political officials to build social service facilities in the neighborhood. We need church pastors to advocate for gang violence offenders in the judicial systems. Continuing to incarcerate youth for gang violence offenses is not the answer. It may be a temporary fix but it's not a permanent, viable solution. We need pastors who will work as mentors in the community and demonstrate love that so many youth desperately long for. We need pastors who can provide social services such as employment opportunities, educational resources, and adequate housing referrals. In other words, we need pastors who take seriously Jesus' radical message of love beyond the church sanctuary, beyond the church council room, beyond the church trustee room, a real love that's none other than radical faith in action.

A dilemma that pastors grapple with is not having the answers. Rev. So-and-So comes to learn that there are no quick fixes or easy solutions to the question of gang violence. Oftentimes, pastors are socialized to believe that they have all the answers and that facilitating a prayer and/or recitations of Bible passages are the key. Wrong! The challenge with clergy being irrelevant and of no use is grounded in a belief that they have the power to "fix" this gang violence problem. Their "fixing" is usually steeped in evangelical rhetoric, admonishing persons to accept a Divine and human Lord and subsequently all their cares will disappear. Unfortunately, pastors must examine the issue of gang violence from a multitude of dynamics—not simply religious. Pastors must take into consideration the social, emotional and existential needs of persons who are involved in gangs and believe gang violence is the answer. The question becomes are you as pastor ready? Are you ready to do real ministry for a real world that's experiencing real pain and needs real hope?

CeaseFire and the Church:
A Partnership Made in Heaven

What can church pastors do to help decrease gang violence? Church pastors can partner with social service organizations in their community. There are several social service organizations that pastors and congregants can join. In Chicago, the social service organization known for producing tangible results is CeaseFire.

CeaseFire is an anti-violence initiative that perceives violence as a "contagious health issue": "Like the infectious diseases in our history, violence is better understood and more successfully treated as an epidemic."[1] CeaseFire's founder, Gary Slutkin, developed groundbreaking research on how gang violence is a health epidemic based on his findings that violence is:

- The #1 cause of death for African Americans and Latino males aged 15–24;

- The #1 cause of death for all people under the age of 34 across many cities;

- The primary reason why more than 1 million people have died in the United States from intentional violence since only 1960.[2]

---

1. "Violence as a Health Issue," http://cureviolence.org/understand-violence/violence-as-a-health-issue.

2. Ibid.

Gang violence also has indirect results. Being exposed to violence has been linked to chronic diseases (heart disease, asthma, stroke, cancer, etc.), mental health issues (PTSD, stress, anxiety, depression, etc.), lower quality of life, and increased risk of perpetuating violence.

CeaseFire employs a three-step methodology of:

- Discovering and interrupting potentially violent encounters;
- Discovering and meeting the needs of persons prone to engaging in violent behaviors;
- Modifying societal standards.

This methodology has contributed to a reduction in violence between 40 and 70 percent.

The CeaseFire initiative implements particular strategies. After discovering violent encounters have occurred, violence "interrupters" or trained workers, report to the hospital where victims are transported to receive medical treatment as well as the community where the incident occurred to calm anxiety and hopefully prevent retaliation. In addition, workers meet with key people in the community about unresolved tensions, recent criminal activity, persons who were recently released from prison into the community and other community concerns. Workers continue ministering to the community to make sure tensions don't rise again around the same violent incident.

Second, trained staff identify particular persons in communities who are considered high-risk or heavily prone to acting out violent behaviors. These trained staff build trust with the high-risk persons by developing a relationship built of mutuality and respect. Next, staff work hard to help high-risk individuals modify their unhealthy violent behaviors. Workers engage in meaningful conversations which seek to deter persons from violent behavior by talking about the results and/or negative impact of violence, offering other healthy, positive solutions instead. Staff also try to give viable, tangible solutions that meet the social needs of high-risk persons such as referrals for employment and/or drug and alcohol recovery.

Last but not least, CeaseFire staff work hard to change the perception of violence in the community. Staff try to organize the community to establish block clubs, tenant councils and neighborhood associations. Staff work with churches to provide social programming that keeps youth engaged and away from negative, unhealthy behaviors. The goal is to create an environment where the norm is based on love.

CeaseFire's work in Chicago has been phenomenal. A recent Northwestern University evaluation showed that reductions in killings went from 41 percent to 73 percent, and a 40 percent reduction in shooting hot spots has occurred.[3] What's most encouraging is that retaliation killings have been totally eliminated in five of eight communities.[4] The evaluation highlighted how "in every program area there was a substantial decline in the median density of shootings following the introduction of CeaseFire."[5]

CeaseFire is picking up steam not only in Chicago but throughout the country. CeaseFire worked in partnership with Johns Hopkins University and the Center for Disease Control to address gang violence in Baltimore. The results included:

- 276 conflict mediations;

- reductions in killings of up to 56% and shootings of up to 44%;

- reductions spread to surrounding communities;

- norms on violence were changed—people in the program were much less likely to accept the use of a gun to settle a dispute; 4 times more likely to show little or no support for gun use.[6]

Similar results were discovered in New York City, where violence has dropped 20 percent as a result of CeaseFire's work.[7]

3. "Scientific Evaluations," https://www.cureviolence.org/results/scientific-evaluations.

4. Ibid.

5. Ibid.

6. Ibid.

7. Ibid.

Churches can partner with CeaseFire in a number of ways. First, church pastors or laypersons could become trained staff of CeaseFire, working as violence "interrupters." This would give the church pastor and/or parishioners an opportunity to actively participate in the happenings of the church community. Also, church memberships can participate in local events sponsored by Cease-Fire in their community. This would portray a message that the faith community actually cares about the community. Last but not least, partnering with CeaseFire gives churches the opportunity to not only care for the spirit of the community but the physical, and emotional component of the community as well, allowing the church to be relevant in the new age. Let's face it. The church is called to be more than simply the spiritual hub of the community. People want more, especially youth. Young people hold the church to be accountable today not only for what happens on Sunday morning but the "going-ons" Monday through Saturday as well.

In 2017, I believe the church's relevancy is on trial. The church's relevancy is standing before twelve jurors. The church's relevancy is standing before a judge. Unfortunately, the church is on the cusp of being handed the death penalty because of all the ways the church has remained silent while violence continues to increasingly ravish our communities.

There is hope, however, and it starts with leadership. Pastors, deacons, trustees and council members must began to do ministry outside the four walls of the church. We must leave the familiar. The comfortable. The safe. We must journey into the deep abyss and talk to "them," "the other," "those people" who we'd rather ignore or worse yet, pretend don't exist. Our memberships are watching. Our communities are watching. Our neighborhoods are watching. Our youth are watching. The life of our beloved institution depends on it.

Chapter 2

A Dream Deferred

The Moment when the Patient Dies

> What happens to a dream deferred?
> Does it dry up
> Like a raisin in the sun?
> Or fester like a sore—
> And then run?
> Does it stink like rotten meat?
> Or crust and sugar over—
> like a syrupy sweet?
> Maybe it just sags
> like a heavy load.
> Or does it explode?
>
> LANGSTON HUGHES

"Caaaarrmmmeeeeen!"

I never heard wailing like this before. Deep painful wailing.

"My sweet baby Carmen!"

She grabbed the small face of the lifeless body. Her tears fell on the still face.

The woman looked like she'd been in a war. Her hair was all over the place. Her eyes were swollen like the after effects of a boxing match. She looked up at me.

"This is my niece Carmen I was telling you about upstairs."

I nodded my head. This is so fucked up. Life is not fair. She's upstairs journeying with her daughter and son-in-law's miscarriage of her much-anticipated grandbaby and now, out of nowhere, she has to deal with the death of her niece. Life is so fucked up.

Carmen's mother stayed in the quiet room with her pastor, while her sister asked to see Carmen's body. We were in the morgue now. Transport had already come to the ER to take the body to the morgue. We aren't allowed to keep a body out past 120 minutes. Also, the nursing staff needed the hospital room for other living patients that needed care. Damn. I hate going to the morgue. It's freezing in here.

"What am I gonna tell my daughter, huh?"

"I understand. This is so hard."

"It's terrible. One girl is no good and now the other one is . . ."

She didn't finish her sentence. Her nose started running. I passed her a box of Kleenex. I thank God I remembered to bring tissue with me down here.

"This is a horrible situation. I get it. I can't imagine how you must be feeling right now."

I'm trying to stay focused on the woman in front of me and not the other four dead bodies that I start imagining in the morgue's freezer. There's nothing else for me to focus my attention on. No pretty pictures. No beautiful lamps. No colorful drywall. Just a dry, brick-framed freezer. No family should be subject to coming down here.

"Who's gonna continue our name?"

"I know this is hard. What did you love most about your niece Carmen?"

"She was funny. . . . Real funny. Great sense of humor."

I smiled.

KNOCK! KNOCK! KNOCK!

"Everything ok chaplain?"

I looked at the public safety officer standing outside peeping his head inside our small freezer room.

"Yes sir. Please give us five more minutes."

You can't go to the morgue by yourself. You must be escorted by a nurse and hospital security officer. And it's not good to stay in the morgue a long time either.

"What are your favorite memories of Carmen?"

She started laughing and crying at the same time. She leaned her head back and stared up at the ceiling. A small smile escaped the corner of her mouth.

"I remember I taught her how to ride a bike. She kept falling down. She would be up riding then next thing you know she'd be down on the ground. When she finally got up and back on her feet, I told her, 'Look, when you start riding again, don't stop. Just keep pedaling. Keep going.' Cuz the only time she'd fall is when she'd look down at her feet."

"That's a beautiful story. Thank you for sharing. What do you think Carmen would say to you in these moments?"

"She'd tell me to stay strong. Don't cry. She'd tell me everything is gonna be ok."

"Everything will be ok, but until then if you wanna cry it's no problem. Go for it. Don't hold it in. Let it out. Then after you cry for a while, hold onto Carmen's words. Everything will be ok."

She nodded her head and started stroking Carmen's forehead.

"How would Carmen want to be remembered?"

"She was hardworking, loving and kind. Even though we hated that she was . . ."

I decided to save her from finishing the statement.

"I understand. Please hold onto that hardworking, loving and kind spirit. Her spirit will never die."

She dropped her head and started crying again.

"You're right."

"I imagine in these moments your niece is saying, 'Keep pedaling auntie. Keep going. Don't look down.'"

She smiled.

"I have to keep pedaling, huh?"

"Yes."

She kissed her niece on the cheek one more time.

"Ok, chaplain, I'm ready to go back to my sister now. See you later my sweet baby. . . . I'm gonna keep going for you. . . ."

When Grief Is Everything You Thought It Wasn't

Grief is hard. Grief is difficult. Grief is unprecedented. It was once believed that grief could occur in stages in which once persons worked through these stages from start to finish in a linear format then they would somehow heal and move forward with their lives never reverting backwards. My work in chaplaincy has proven this to not be the case. There are no linear stages to work through, but I prefer to see these stages as circular, meaning one can start at denial, then shift to anger, then shift back to denial, then go back to anger, then move to acceptance, then go to bargaining and maybe shift back to acceptance only to go back to denial. Depending on the type of loss, there's no ever "getting over it." For example, I've discovered in my work in this field, that the loss of child is never "accepted." Parents grieve permanently and eternally for the rest of their lives.

Grief is also impacted by the formalities and policies surrounding the death process in a hospital. For example, when a patient dies in a hospital, the chaplain journeys with the family to complete what we call "death paperwork" such as a Release of Body form, Organ Donation form, and/or autopsy form. Completing this paperwork with a grieving family must be handled with care and sensitivity. The grief process is further impacted by the "external" interdisciplinary team such as the local law enforcement or county medical examiner's office. When a person comes into the hospital and dies within twenty-four hours of presenting to the hospital, oftentimes nursing and medical staff must report the death to the local police department who then contact the county medical examiner's office to determine if a formal investigation, including autopsy, needs to take place. The chaplain can play the role of gentle liaison between the family and other counterparts.

In the grief process, self-care is pivotal. Encouraging survivors of loss to practice physically, mentally and spiritually healthy habits is key to survivors achieving hope and stability. There are many forms of self-care that exist. Self-care can include a walk through a park, adopting a pet, gardening, joining a social service organization or practicing yoga. I will speak further about self-care in the final chapter of this book.

I am a big proponent of inviting grieving persons to participate in counseling and support groups. Allow me to add a caveat. I do not support spiritual counseling, but professional mental health counseling to deal with grief and loss. Spiritual counseling asks persons to consider where the Divine is in the midst of their grief. Unfortunately, grieving persons do not need to discover the Divine so much as they need to discover the mental, emotional and psychological feelings and dynamics associated with their grief. Persons need to explore past life experiences and the impact of those experiences on their current being. Thus, professional mental health counseling is deeply necessary. Oftentimes, I'm saddened when grieving persons use spiritual counseling somewhat like a band-aid or rug to simply cover up the difficult emotional feelings that they want to hide or pretend don't exist.

Professional counseling allows persons the opportunity to work through the life review process:

- What did your loved one do well?
- What were your loved one's growing edges or shortcomings?
- What can you learn from those growing edges or shortcomings?
- How can you use your loved one's life to inspire you?
- If your loved one was here, what would he/she say to you?
- How can you remember and live your loved one's legacy?
- What's helpful for you to not get stuck in the loss of your loved one?

Think about your own life. Reflect on your own life experiences. If you were to die today, what would be said about you? If you could conduct a life review of your own life what important messages would stand out? Would you have a legacy that would be remembered?

CHAPTER 3

Connection Is Key

"GOOD MORNING, CHAPLAIN."

I look up from reading my census sheets and notice a nurse crossing my path.

"Hello. How was your weekend?"

"It was wonderful. We had a great time at church yesterday."

In these moments I remember that my role as chaplain is to also provide a supportive presence to staff. They work so hard, especially the nurses. It's nice for them to have someone to talk to as well.

"I'm happy to hear that. What happened?"

"We had our annual Women's Day service. We had a famous woman preacher from Texas as our guest speaker."

I stop to talk to the nurse for a moment to also calm my own anxiety. I must admit, I am a bit nervous to walk into the patient's room.

"Cool. What did she preach about?"

"She preached about dry bones in, huh . . ."

"Ezekiel?"

"Yes, Ezekiel. It was a good sermon. But my favorite part of the service was the dance selection by the praise dancers. Those young ladies are so talented."

"Yes, they are. I saw them before at another church and they were fantastic. They move with such grace and lots of charisma."

"You're right."

"Well, I must go now."

"See you later."

I say a prayer, recite the Isaiah 41:10 passage to myself, then I walk to the patient's door and lightly knock.

"Come in."

"Hello, Mr. Carlos."

"Hi."

"My name is Danielle and I am the unit chaplain. I just came by to check on you. Is there anything I can do for you this morning?"

"No, I'm fine."

"Ok, I'll stop by a little later. Take care."

"You too. Thank you."

I never expect a patient to open up and talk on my first visit. Usually this doesn't happen until the third of fourth visit. I believe the initial visits are laying the groundwork and building trust in the patient-chaplain encounter. Most people would be scared to keep visiting the gang member patients. So they visit one time then check the patient off their census list. Thus, continuous visits show I actually care and want to have an engaging patient-chaplain relationship. That afternoon, I visit the patient again.

"Hi, Mr. Carlos. How are you feeling this afternoon?"

"I'm in a lot of pain. My hand is hurting so bad."

He raises his hand and looks at it in disgust.

"Has your nurse given you your afternoon pain medicine?"

"Yes, but it doesn't seem like its working. I paged the nurse but she told me to try sleeping."

"I'm sorry you are in pain right now. I'll leave you alone though so you can rest."

"Thank you."

The next day, I visit the patient again.

"Good morning, Mr. Carlos."

"Good morning."

"Are you feeling better today?"

"Yes, but my hand still hurts and my leg has this tingling feeling."

"Hmmm."

I look at the patient with a sense of empathy.

"I can't wait to get home. I'm going to . . ."

The phone rings.

"I'll step out so you can talk alone."

"No. Please wait a minute."

The patient answers the phone. I take a step back from his bed and survey his room. It's empty except for a huge "Get Well" balloon floating in the air. Next to the balloon is a card which is standing upright on the tray table. It says, "Get Well Soon From Mom." "I'll call you back. I'm talking to a lady from the hospital right now."

The patient quickly ends the conversation and sets his phone on a nearby night stand. He adjusts his pillow and pulls himself up in the bed.

"Do you need any help?"

"No, I can do it."

He sets himself up in the bed.

"Who did you say you were again?"

"I am the chaplain for this floor."

"What's that?"

"It's like a hospital minister."

"What do you do?"

"Technically, I visit patients and share a message of encouragement with them while they are here in the hospital. But most of the time, I provide a listening ear if a patient ever wants to talk."

"Do you ever tell somebody else what a patient shared with you?"

"Never. I keep all conversations confidential."

"Oh, ok. . . . You want to hear about what happened to me?"

"Sure. May I sit down?"

"Yes."

I sit in one of the patient's chairs near his bed. He begins to tell me a long story about his encounter. I listen with empathy. No judgments. No condemnation. After he tells me the story, he looks at me with frustration and sadness.

"So, I got shit to handle now."

"What do you want to do now?"

"I got business now."

"What are you gonna do?"

"Sorry, boss lady, I can't tell you that."

"Ok, I understand."

A moment of silence goes by. I break the silence with a question.

"Can I ask you a question?"

"Sure."

"Have you ever been in a situation like this before?"

The patient goes quiet. After a few moments he answers.

"Yeah . . . why?"

"What happened?"

"I was walking home from school. I stopped at a corner to talk with some friends from my neighborhood. A car came speeding down the street. A boy was hanging out of one of the windows. He pulled out a gun and started shooting at me and my friends."

"Are you serious?"

I sit upright in my chair and tilt my head slightly.

"Yes. We all started running in different directions."

"I can't imagine what was going through your mind."

"I was scared. But I started running as fast as I could. I don't even know where I was going, I was just trying to get far away from that car. As I was running, I looked down and noticed blood dripping from my leg."

"You didn't feel any pain?"

"No, but when I saw the blood running down my leg, I realized I was shot and I fell on the ground."

"You probably went into shock. That happens to many of our patients after they realize they've been shot."

"That's what must have happened to me. I don't remember what happened after that. My brother told me later that an old lady from inside one of the houses saw me fall on the ground and she called 911."

"So, let me get this straight . . ."

I retold the patient's story, highlighting major points and memorable events.

"Thank God that lady saw you."

"Yes, the man upstairs was definitely looking out for me."

"You're right."

"Now, I have to get home. My buddies know who did this and we have to take care of our business."

"Where is God now?"

He reflects for a minute.

"Hmmmm. . . . I never thought about that. I suppose he's with me now like he was before."

"You seem like a pretty smart young man. Why do you feel the need to belong to a gang?"

"Well, I like having friends to hang out with and they are the only people who really understand me. I can depend on them. My brother works long hours and is hardly ever home. But I can hang out with my buddies and there's always somebody with me."

"I'm sorry that you feel lonely sometimes."

"Don't be sorry. I've always got my boys by my side. That's why when I get out the hospital we're going to take care of our business."

"What do you mean?"

"You know, 'Eye for an eye, tooth for a tooth.'"

"Before you start thinking about all of that, concentrate on making a full recovery."

"Oh most definitely, then I'm going to take care of my business."

"I'm going to get ready and leave now."

I stand up from the chair. Before I leave I ask another reflective question.

"Can you do me a favor though?"

"What is it?"

I pick up the small Bible lying on the patient's table.

"Can you read this passage for me?"

I point out Isaiah 41:10.

"Tomorrow I will come visit you again."

"The doctors said I'm going home tomorrow."

"I know. I'm going to visit you before you are discharged. Let me know what you think about this scripture."

"Ok."

"Thank you, goodbye."

The third day, I visit the patient for one final time.

"Hello, Mr. Carlos."

"Hey. You know you can just call me Juan. That's my first name."

"Thank you, Juan."

"You know I thought about the passage you asked me to read in that Bible."

"Oh cool. What did you think about it?"

"It sounded good. The man talking was God?"

"Yes. He was letting a group of people, who were in a bad situation, know that he was with them and he would grant them justice."

"Does this scripture say anything to you?"

He thinks for a minute. Then he drops his head.

"Maybe God can do the same for me?"

The patient is quiet for a moment.

"How is God going to give me justice? Only my boys can handle that."

"Hey, speaking of your boys . . . have they come by to visit you?"

"No."

"Has anybody come by to visit you?"

"The only person who's been by to visit is my brother."

He points to the balloon and the card. He passes me the card. On the inside of the card is a handwritten letter from Juan's older brother, expressing his frustrations with his unhealthy lifestyle.

"The guys may not have come by, but I really depend on them. My brother has to work all the time to pay the bills. I want to get a job to help out, but I can't. So my brother has to be away from home all day and work overtime to support us. He's never at home. Then when he comes home, he has to cook and clean and take care of the house. I hang out with the guys because they're always around."

"Sounds like you have a great resource at home."

"Who, my brother?"

I remain quiet.

"Do your friends have older siblings who take care of them?"

"No."

He remains quiet again. I interject.

"What does justice look like for you?"

"I don't want to have to struggle anymore. I want a good job."

"What are you good at doing?"

"I like to help people."

"Aw, that sounds awesome."

"How about getting a job where you can help people?"

"Yeah, I've always wanted to be a firefighter!"

"What's stopping you?"

"I need to get my GED then I need to take a couple of classes to get certified."

"So what's stopping you?"

"I guess nothing."

He thinks for a minute then he interjects.

"If I was a firefighter I could help my brother out financially and do something I love. . . . I probably wouldn't have time for my dudes anymore either."

He thinks for another moment. My mind begins to wonder. He interrupts my thoughts.

"Then I wouldn't have to worry about getting shot at. . . . I wouldn't be in this life anymore."

He pauses for another moment. Then he has an aha moment.

"Maybe God's way of giving me justice is me having a job doing something I really love, making money for me and my brother and keeping me from getting killed?"

"Yes. I could see that!"

"Me too."

"Listen, Juan. You seem to me to be very smart and intelligent. You are so caring and loving. I can really tell. I think you'd be a great firefighter."

Tears start rolling down his face.

"I'll talk to you later, boss lady."

"Ok, feel free to call me at the hospital whenever you want to talk."

"Sure. Thanks."

A Transforming Encounter

During the summer months of my chaplain residency at Advocate Christ Medical Center, I met a young man named Juan Carlos,[1] a 21-year-old Hispanic male from the southeast side of Chicago. Juan Carlos had come into the hospital as a result of a fight between members of his gang, the Latin Kings, and individuals from a rival street organization. Juan Carlos had been shot and fortunately, his injuries were not life threatening. During his stay, I visited Juan Carlos on several occasions and we only chatted briefly on each occasion. He never wanted to engage in any lengthy or detailed conversations. Therefore, I just stopped by his room everyday, while making my rounds, to check on him and let him know I was available if he ever needed a chaplain.

On Juan Carlos' last day of being in the hospital, I stopped by to make my final visit and wish him God's blessings on his journey to full recovery at home. After talking briefly about his discharge, he brought up the scripture (Isaiah 41:10) that I asked him to read and reflect on the day before. It reads: "So do not fear, for I am with you; do not be dismayed, for I am your God. I will strengthen you and help you; I will uphold you with my righteous right hand."[2] This scripture is featured on a painting located in Christ Hospital's main chapel. Juan Carlos went on to reflect about what the scripture meant to him. Two points seemed to resonate with him.

1. Individual's name has been changed to protect his identity.
2. Isaiah 41:10.

First, the phrase "I am with you" in this Isaiah text reminded him of God's love for him. Second, the statement "I will uphold you with my righteous right hand" encouraged him that God would grant justice on his behalf. However, he stated that he had problems understanding how God would grant him justice. From his perspective, Juan Carlos saw justice in the form of his assailants, the rival gang members who shot him, being arrested and jailed. On the other hand, he understood that the possibilities of this occurring were probably impossible given the circumstances of the incident (i.e., there were no credible eyewitnesses to the incident) and his lack of faith in the criminal justice system.

While Juan Carlos was talking, I also had the voice of his older brother in my head. After reading the card from Juan's brother, I was able to understand his brother's feelings. Juan's brother had disappointments with his younger brother's lifestyle. As the card stated, the older sibling was frustrated with Juan Carlos' choice to join the gang. In the card, the older sibling expressed his fear of losing his younger brother to gang violence, citing his great love for his brother. The older sibling also discussed in the card his frustrations with Juan Carlos' reasoning for joining the Latin Kings street gang. With the two brothers' parents inactive in their lives and the elder sibling carrying much of the responsibility in supporting his little brother, Juan Carlos joined the gang to earn money to support himself from the gang's illegal drug sales. However, in the card the older sibling repeatedly expressed his younger brother's lack of need for the street gang given the older brother's new second job. From Juan Carlos' perspective, he didn't want to be a burden to his older brother, nor did he feel comfortable accepting what he deemed "financial handouts." So, Juan Carlos turned to the Latin Kings for financial stability to solve his and his older brother's poverty woes and to cure his feelings of abandonment and lack of love from his parents. With these thoughts racing through his mind, Juan Carlos struggled to understand how and when God would be just in his life.

I invited Juan Carlos to reflect on God's justice from another perspective. The righteousness or justice of God only comes through the actions of human beings. When God wanted to be just toward oppressed Cubans, the Divine worked through the actions of Che Guevara. When God wanted to be just toward oppressed African Americans, the Divine worked through the actions of Martin Luther King Jr. Likewise, I shared with Juan Carlos that when God wanted to be loving and just toward him, the Divine worked through the actions of his older brother. I shared with Juan Carlos that God's love for him was revealed through the love of his older brother. God responded to Juan Carlos' feelings of abandonment by sending the elder sibling to provide that love and nurture that Juan Carlos desperately needed. Also, I encouraged Juan Carlos to develop a new identity apart from the gang such as a budding career as a firefighter which could possibly be God's "righteous right hand" providing deliverance from his active gang membership. Money gained from Juan's new identity and employment could be the substitute for money gained through the gang's illegal drug sales.

Racial and Socioeconomic Factors

Juan Carlos challenged me to become more aware of the sociological factors which fostered his feelings of alienation. To be more specific, Juan Carlos verbalized how racism and classism in American society against Hispanic and African American youth / young adult males keep them from living productive lives which, in turn, fosters feelings of being alienated from the greater society.

Before the hospital chaplain enters the room of a gang member patient, he or she must be socially aware of their patients' experiences in American society. For example, my encounter with Juan Carlos forced me to research the effects of racism and classism on Hispanic youth. According to the National Gang Center, Hispanic/Latino and black/African Americans make up 80 percent of the racial/ethnic demographic of gang membership from 1996–2011.[3]

According to a survey completed in the early 2000s era by the University of Chicago's Center for the Study of Race, Politics

3. National Gang Center, "National Youth Gang Survey Analysis: Demographics," https://www.nationalgangcenter.gov/survey-analysis/demographics.

and Culture, 45 percent of Hispanic youth believe "it's hard to get ahead because you face so much discrimination."[4] In fact, 30 percent of Hispanic youth think "you have to act white to get ahead."[5] In order to understand Juan Carlos' feelings of alienation, I had to have some background knowledge of his sociological experiences. I had to be mindful of how many Hispanic males, in comparison to their white counterparts, suffer from poverty, inadequate education, unemployment, incarceration and sickness and diseases. The sociological factors of racism and classism against Hispanic and African American youth play a key role in why these particular youth, who belong to gangs, experience feelings of alienation.

However, other groups of people who are not Hispanic or African American but who belong to gangs also experience feelings of alienation. It is important to note that gang members are not only Hispanic or African American. For example, most white gangs consist of Skinheads or Ku Klux Klan groups. White youth in gangs, such as the KKK or Skinheads, feel alienated from the larger society because, from their perspective, so many benefits and opportunities (i.e., affirmative action) are granted to non-whites. Add to that the fact that from 2008 to 2016 the president of the United States, Barack Obama, is African American. "They strongly feel that the government—that their white forefathers established, fought, and died for—today gives preferential treatment to minorities and illegal aliens," according to Richard Valdemar, a retired sergeant from the Los Angeles County Sheriff's Department who spent most of his thirty-three years on the job combating gangs.[6] Also many white youth gangs believe there is generally a negative perception of white people, in American society, given white people's history of marginalization against non-white groups. According to Valdemar, "The system seems to tolerate Black, Hispanic, Asian, and Native American racists and radicals but loves to hate the Whites and especially the Nazis."[7]

4. Cohen et al., "Attitudes and Behavior," 18.
5. Ibid.
6. Valdemar, "Skinhead and Other White Supremacist Gangs."
7. Ibid.

Other types of gangs formulated based on ethnicity also experience feelings of alienation, such as Asian gangs: "Before 1975, Asian gangs were largely limited to disaffected Chinese youth living in the Chinatown of larger cities. Such youth, alienated from the greater community, were also largely marginalizes within the Chinese community itself due to a variety of social and economic conditions. . . . Since that time, the image of Asian gangs has changed to include new immigrant groups, such as Vietnamese, Vietnamese-Chinese, Laotian, Cambodian and Hmong gangs, which can now be found in communities across the nation where recent Southeast Asian immigrants have settled," according to Valdemar.[8] All of this is to say that it is the role of the hospital chaplain and parish clergy, before engaging gang member patients, to become socially aware of why these particular groups would feel alienated against in society.

The Impact of African Enslavement on African American Gang Members and Gang Violence in the United States

There are three major time periods in history that have impacted African Americans tremendously and created long-lasting psychological results:

- African Enslavement (1619–1865)
- Segregation (1865–1954)
- Mass Incarceration (1954–present)

These three time periods were distinctly based on racism and contribute to the psychological damage that has given way to the creation of African American gangs and self-hatred that fosters gang violence. Of these three time periods, I believe African enslavement has had the most profound affect on African Americans and is the core reason African American gangs act out violence.

African enslavement first began when a badly damaged Dutch ship, called the White Lion, carrying about twenty African

8. Ibid.

persons who were kidnapped from their continent crashed on the shores of Jamestown, Virginia, in 1619.[9] Colonists residing in the Chesapeake Bay of Virginia bartered food and services in exchange for the African human cargo on the ship. These persons were "sold" like property and forced to provide free labor tending to massive farms, picking hundreds of crops per day and physically erecting various gigantic homes and businesses. Work conditions were exhausting, grueling and extremely difficult to say the least. Persons worked under the treacherous hot sun and were not allotted necessary break times or much-needed medical attention, basic sick leave, and essential time off.

Owners instituted a color caste system that still affects African Americans today. African persons with a lighter hue were thought to be "good negroes" or better than persons with a darker skin tone. These "good negroes" were forced to work in inhumane, debilitating conditions inside their owners' homes, cooking, cleaning and being at the arduous beck and call of white families and guests. This created an internalized hatred among African persons whereby darker-complected Africans became jealous and envious of lighter complected Africans, believing that those who worked "in the house" had easier lifestyles in comparison to those who worked "in the fields" outside.

Persons both inside the home and outside the home were physically beaten and emotionally traumatized if they didn't perform duties quickly and thoroughly. Oftentimes, if they didn't complete tasks as demanded by sadistic owners, persons were tied to "whipping posts" or trees in which they would be struck repeatedly with painful leather belts. They were no longer called by their given names of origin, but they were simply referred to as "slaves."

There was also much sexual trauma instituted against African persons during this time. For example, white slave masters would repeatedly rape African women and sometimes African men whenever they felt sexual desires to do so, or white slave masters would force African persons, both women and men, to commit

---

9. "Slavery in America," History.com (2009), http://www.history.com/topics/black-history/slavery.

atrocious sexual acts. Owners would "breed" African persons like animals, forcing any African person to have sexual relations with any African woman. Oftentimes, owners would force African men to engage in sexual acts with and impregnate their own biological female relatives. Sometimes, these female relatives would be an African male's own mother or even underage daughter.

African persons also suffered the destruction of kinship ties and a sense of community as a result of the callous and brutal auction block. The auction block was a market space where African persons were brought or sold between white owners who would make monetary bids on the Africans' bodies. On the auction block, African persons were stripped completely naked for hundreds of onlookers to see. Examiners would pick and prod African persons' genital areas like an inspection prior to bidding. Most disheartening was the fact that biological African families were forever torn apart as white owners could bid and buy individual family members. The auction block was the sight and sound of much loud screaming and deep, deep wailing as wives were permanently separated from husbands and children were permanently separated from mothers. Nancy Boyd-Franklin writes: "Slave masters attempted to destroy the kinship bonds and the cultural system of Black Africans."[10] Boyd-Franklin goes on to highlight:

> Slave masters utilized a dehumanizing process that attempted to deprive the African men and women of their traditions—including family ties, language, customs, food and spiritual rituals. African people were brought to this country to be bought and sold, according to each individual slave's market value, to his or her suitability for a particular region and/or task. Slaves thus often lost family members to the expanding market or to early death. Since slave masters were only required to provide slaves with the barest essentials for survival, life expectancies were low and mortality was high.[11]

10. Boyd-Franklin, *Black Families in Therapy*, 9.
11. Ibid.

White slave owners also manipulated African persons' spirituality. White slave masters would not allow African persons to practice their own religious views anymore. Instead, white slave masters forced African persons to become fully indoctrinated with the Christian faith tradition and the most importantly, Christianity's sacred text, the Bible. Oftentimes, evil-spirited white slave masters would read certain Bible passages to African persons while they were being beaten on the whipping posts or sold on the auction blocks.

White slave owners attempted to spiritually justify slavery by citing biblical scriptures and that would convince African persons that God actually ordained slavery. As an example, white slave masters would quote the story of Ham (Genesis 9:25) or the Leviticus code (Leviticus 25:44–46) or passages from the New Testament such as Apostle Paul admonishing slaves to obey their masters in Ephesians or the book of Philemon, where Paul encourages a runaway slave to go back home to his master. According to Kelly Brown Douglas, one pro-slavery minister often preached:

> Our Lord repeatedly spoke of slaves especially in several of his parables, without the slightest intimation that he condemned slavery, and in such a way as plainly showed that he considered it lawful. . . . We are told, Matt. 8:23–35, that a Centurion came to Jesus beseeching him to heal his sick servant. . . . If the holding of slaves had been sinful, Jesus would, we doubt not, have informed [the Centurion].[12]

African persons tried to combat these messages through encouraging hymns, spirituals and liberating theological exegesis of the Christian biblical text. African persons tried to compare their plight to the children of Israel suffering in Egypt, believing one day that God would send them a Moses to set them free (Exodus). They sang such spirituals as:

> When the children were in bondage,
> They cried unto the Lord,
> To turn back Pharaoh's army,

12. Douglas, *Black Christ*, 15.

He turned back Pharaoh's army,
When Pharaoh crossed the water,
The waters came together,
And drowned ole Pharaoh's army,
Hallelu![13]

Slavery was legalized in 1641 and by 1860 more than one million African persons had been shipped from Africa to the United States.[14] Unfortunately, the country was growing divided by the topic of slavery. States primarily in the Southern part of the county supported slavery, while many states in the Northern region did not. Hence, many Northern states became "free states," where slaves from the South could escape and gain freedom. The growing unrest over the subject of slavery spurred the Civil War, which suffered the most casualties of any other war on US soil.[15] On January 1, 1863, President Abraham Lincoln ended the debate, and subsequent Civil War, regarding slavery by signing the Emancipation Proclamation.[16] Unfortunately, many Southern states continued secretly keeping African persons in bondage, so June 19, 1865, federal troops arrived in Galveston, Texas, to enforce the Emancipation Proclamation.[17] June 19, now known as "Juneteenth," is recognized as the authentic Emancipation Proclamation. The Thirteenth Amendment was added to the US Constitution, officially abolishing slavery.

Because our kinship ties were broken and we were deprived of our traditions during the period of African enslavement, I believe African Americans feel psychologically and spiritually drawn to join gangs and commit gang violence, because at the core we don't love ourselves, we don't love each other and we don't believe that God loves us. African enslavement laid the ground work to the segregation / Jim Crow period. I believe that African enslavement created an inferiority complex among Africans and their

13. Ibid., 26–27.

14. "Slavery in America," History.com.

15. Crigger and Santhanam, "How Many Americans Have Died."

16. "Slavery in America," History.com.

17. Ibid.

descendents, now termed African Americans. This inferiority complex inhibits us from believing in ourselves. We don't even compete in the race because we refuse to even approach the starting line, believing that we are unfit to be in the race to begin with or even have the competency or skills to run. Our inferiority complex is compromised even further through our government's lack of acknowledgment about the atrocities of African enslavement and by a refusal to grant reparations. Our inferiority complex keeps us from loving ourselves so we hurt ourselves by engaging in unhealthy behaviors such as drug, alcohol, sexual, and gambling addictions. Our inferiority complex sabotages our self-care. We limit physical activity and refuse to seek mental health treatment for emotional needs. Our inferiority complex robs us of our hopes and dreams. We don't seek educational achievements or career advancements. Our inferiority complex makes us fearful and ashamed to go to the next level of self improvement or it makes us content with our current mediocre status quo. We come to believe that gang membership is the epitome of life.

Our lack of love for ourselves also inhibits our ability to love others. We find ourselves in an entangled web of either competing with others or demonstrating complete disregard for others' existence. The effects of African enslavement enable us to act like crabs in a bucket in which we hate to see others progress so we'd rather pull others down so they can stay on an equal level with us. Our capitalistic way of life holds us back from caring for others, but rather imparts in us a belief that we live life solo, alone and that we don't need anybody to survive. We see others as competition rather than community. We live lives afraid that others will take from us and victimize our resources.

Worse yet, we ignore the pain of others and maybe even pretend that they don't exist. We wave our fingers at people, believing that it's not our problem if our neighbor is suffering. We embrace a "pull yourself up by your bootstraps" mentality ("if I got mine, you can get yours"). We act out judgments against people, chastising them for external circumstances beyond their control that forced them into difficult predicaments. We participate in acts of gang violence because we believe that gang violence is not morally or ethically wrong because we live in an "every man/woman for himself/herself" society or we misquote Malcolm X, saying the way of life is "eye for an eye, tooth for a tooth." We live in a microwave society which says we don't have to work hard for success, but it's automatically owed to us and/or therefore we can take it from somebody or something else right now without breaking a sweat. We believe that gang violence is not our problem because it involves "those people over there." We miss the correlations between how our circumstances directly and indirectly impact the circumstances of others.

African enslavement also impacted our religious beliefs. We have a deep sense of spirituality but we no longer have a loyal conviction to religion. This is why the black church is dying. The black church was once the hub of African American life, culture and community. However, as we become more conscious of our African history, we find it increasingly difficult to reconcile the Christian church of our African ancestors with the Christian church of our white slave masters. Denominationalism is dying. Fortunately, spirituality is rising. We believe that God is with us. We hear God's voice in other mediums outside the walls of the church. We are reminded of the providence of an omnipotent God in hip hop songs like Kendrick Lamar's "Alright":

> Alls my life I has to fight, nigga
> Alls my life I . . .
> Hard times like, "God!"
> Bad trips like, "Yeah!"
> Nazareth, I'm fucked up
> Homie, you fucked up
> But if God got us, then we gon' be alright . . .[18]

It's time for the church to be resurrected. It's time for our self-esteem and pride to be resurrected. It's time for our sense of community and communal ties to be resurrected. We don't have

---

18. "Alright," lyrics at http://genius.com/Kendrick-lamar-alright-lyrics.

to continue to be paralyzed by our past pain we experienced during the period of African enslavement. While this pain has been passed down from generation to generation, our future is not deterministic. There is hope. We can take the lessons from our past and transform them into strength for the future. All is not lost. We can break barriers for our future offspring. Our future generations need us to lay pivotal groundwork today. What are you called to do in these moments? Is there something that's been burning in your heart to do but fear and shame stop you? It's time to come out from your hiding space. Is there a new outreach program that can touch the lives of others that's been formulating in your mind but you keep putting it off? It's time for new beginnings. Have you been grappling with your faith? It's ok to start over again, fresh and new. What's your identity? What's your calling and purpose? What mission has God uniquely designed just for you? Are you walking in the authority of your full identity? Are you walking in the potential of your full calling? Today, is your new Day. Your dawn is calling.

Culture of Violence in the United States

It's hard to discuss the topic of gang violence in the United States without talking about our current culture of violence that we live in today. We are consumed by violence in America. Violence is all around us. No wonder youth feel drawn to acting out violent behaviors. Violence has been embedded in the fabric of our society. It's in our movies, our music videos, our politics, our law enforcement, our video games and even our religion.

According to IMDb, *The Godfather* (1972) is the second-highest-rated movie in the United States of all time behind *The Shawshank Redemption* (1994), which rates as number one.[19] Both movies glorify violence. *The Shawshank Redemption*, staring Tim Robbins and Morgan Freeman, tells the story of two imprisoned men who form a deep friendship over several years, discovering peace and eventually redemption from their violent pasts. In 1995,

19. IMDb Charts, Top Rated Movies, http://www.imdb.com/chart/top.

this gruesome movie was nominated for seven Oscars and scored sixteen other movie awards.

The Godfather, staring an all-star cast including Marlon Brando and Al Pacino, highlights an aging patriarch of an organized crime dynasty transferring control of his clandestine empire to his reluctant son. The Godfather has become an unofficial guidebook for many street gangs. The movie spun into a series and also gave way for the development of other organized crime and violence-ridden movies such as Goodfellas (1990), Carlito's Way (1993), and Pulp Fiction (1994).

In addition to movies, music videos have also grown increasingly violent and glorify violent lifestyles that influence gang members and contribute to our progressively violent culture. Oftentimes, rap music penned by African American male hip hop artists is stereotyped as the most violent music of all time. However this is not true. According to the Dallas Observer, the ten most violent music videos of all time are rock music videos primarily produced by European American males.[20]

According to the American Psychological Association, "songs with violent lyrics increase aggression related thoughts and emotions and this effect is directly related to the violence in the lyrics":

> In a series of five experiments involving over 500 college students, researchers from Iowa State University and the Texas Department of Human Services examined the effects of seven violent songs by seven artists and eight nonviolent songs by seven artists. The students listened to the songs and were given various psychological tasks to measure aggressive thoughts and feelings. One such task involved participants classifying words that can have both aggressive and nonaggressive meanings, such as rock and stick.[21]

20. McCann, "30 Most Disturbing Songs of All Time."

21. "Violent Music Lyrics Increase Aggressive Thoughts and Feelings, according to New Study," APA press release, May 4, 2003, http://www.apa.org/news/press/releases/2003/05/violent-songs.aspx.

Discovering that the subjects were more aggressive and hostile, "one major conclusion from this and other research on violent entertainment media is that content matters," said Dr. Craig Anderson, who also added: "This message is important for all consumers, but especially for parents of children and adolescents."[22]

Our never-ending engagement in military conflict/war is another contributing factor to our American culture of violence. To date, we have facilitated air strikes of thirteen countries in the last sixty-nine years.[23] Those thirteen countries are Korea, Vietnam, Cambodia, Laos, Grenada, Panama, Iraq, Somalia, Bosnia, Kosovo, Afghanistan, Libya, and now Syria. There is no country that has engaged in this same amount of military conflict. Thus, we have become desensitized to violence abroad. We move on with our lives from day to day sometimes even forgetting we are at war. The results are damaging. From the Revolutionary War to our current War on Terror, more than 1.1 million Americans have been killed in all US wars.[24] We've also spent some pretty hefty bucks as well:

- Total War Funding: $1.64 trillion has been allocated through the Overseas Contingency Operations (war) fund, including $73.3 billion in fiscal year 2015.

- Iraq: $817.8 billion has been allocated for the war in Iraq since 2003, including an estimated $1.0 billion in fiscal year 2015.

- Afghanistan: $714.8 billion has been allocated for the war in Afghanistan since 2001, including $35.1 billion in fiscal year 2015.

- ISIS: $6.2 billion has been allocated to fight the Islamic State (also known as ISIS or ISIL), including $5.4 billion in fiscal year 2015.

- Pentagon Slush Fund: Overseas Contingency Operations has been used to funnel a conservatively estimated $100.9 billion

22. Ibid.

23. Linker, "Why America Can't Break Out."

24. Crigger and Santhanam, "How Many Americans Have Died."

in non-war spending to the Pentagon to avoid legislated budget caps, including an estimated $30 billion in fiscal year 2015.[25]

Our culture of violence has also been impacted by the rising number of shocking recorded videos of police brutality significantly involving white police officers and African American males. While police brutality has been a silent epidemic swept under the rug for many years, these heinous cases have made national news and gained global attention with the invention of cell phone cameras providing indisputable evidence. According to Mapping Police Violence, a research collaborative collecting comprehensive data on police killings nationwide to quantify the impact of police violence in communities, in 2015, police killed more than one hundred unarmed black people.[26] Other key findings included:

- Nearly 1 in 3 black people killed by police in 2015 were identified as unarmed, though the actual number is likely higher due to underreporting.

- 37% of unarmed people killed by police were black in 2015 despite black people being only 13% of the US population.

- Unarmed black people were killed at 5 times the rate of unarmed whites in 2015.

- Only 10 of the 102 cases in 2015 where an unarmed black person was killed by police resulted in officer(s) being charged with a crime, and only 2 of these deaths (Matthew Ajibade and Eric Harris) resulted in convictions of officers involved. Only 1 of 2 officers convicted for their involvement in Matthew Ajibade's death received jail time. He was sentenced to 1 year in jail and allowed to serve this time exclusively on weekends. Deputy Bates, who killed Eric Harris, will be sentenced May 31.[27]

25. "Cost of National Security Counters," National Priorities Projct, updated May 28, 2015, https://www.nationalpriorities.org/cost-of/resources/notes-and-sources.

26. Mapping Police Violence, https://mappingpoliceviolence.org/unarmed.

27. Ibid.

Within the last five years there have been several high-profile police brutality cases that have spurred massive protests, rallies, and demonstrations nationwide, including:

- Waller County, TX: Sandra Bland, 28, was pulled over for a routine traffic stop, which the deputy quickly escalated by removing Sandra from the vehicle and physically restraining her. She would later die in a jail cell under dubious circumstances. Trooper Brian Encina was charged with perjury for lying about the events leading up to Sandra's arrest.

- Baltimore, MD: Freddie Gray died from injuries sustained during a prolonged ride in a police van while handcuffed and shackled on the floor. He was arrested after catching the eye of a police officer and running away. Six officers were charged with crimes including murder for killing Freddie, but all the officers were acquitted.

- North Charleston, SC: Walter Scott was pulled over by North Charleston police officer Michael Slager for a minor traffic violation. Scott fled but Slager caught up with him and attempted to deploy his Taser. The Taser was not effective and as Scott ran away, Slager opened fire. The final altercation was caught on video. Officer Slager has been charged with murder for killing Walter.

- Cleveland, OH: Tamir Rice was in a park playing with a BB gun. A caller reported that a male was pointing a pistol at random people, stating twice that the gun was "probably fake." Police pulled up within 10 feet from Tamir and shot him two seconds later in the abdomen. Neither officer administered first aid, instead arresting Tamir's sister who rushed to his aid. Tamir didn't received first aid until four minutes later from a deputy who was nearby. He died soon after. He was 12 years old.

- Beavercreek, OH: John Crawford III was killed after police were called to a Walmart for reports of a man walking through the store with a rifle. It wasn't a real gun but a BB gun from the store. He was 22 years old.

- Cleveland, OH: Tanisha Anderson suffered from schizophrenia, and officers agreed with the family that she should be taken to a medical center for evaluation. When officers cuffed Anderson and tried to place her inside their vehicle she allegedly resisted. Officers then tasered her and tackled her to the ground, forcing her head onto the ground. Anderson became unresponsive and was pronounced dead at the hospital. She was 37 years old.

- Ferguson, MO: Michael Brown Jr. had either battered a police officer or was innocently walking down the street with a friend. Witnesses say he was unarmed, with his hands in the air, and the officer shot him more than eight times. Even after a grand jury hearing, details are unclear. Brown's death touched off months of protests around the United States. Brown was 18 years old.

- Staten Island, NY: Eric Garner, a father and grandfather, died after Officer Daniel Pantaleo put him in a chokehold and other officers slammed his head against the sidewalk, video of the incident shows. Garner could be heard saying, "I can't breathe," repeatedly while the officer continued to apply the chokehold, eventually killing him. The police officers suspected Garner of selling untaxed cigarettes. No charges were filed against the officers responsible. He was 43 years old.[28]

Many organizations have scrambled to highlight these atrocities and more importantly bring legislative change—one such organization is #BlackLivesMatter (BLM), a network founded by Patrisse Cullors, Opal Tometi, and Alicia Garza.[29] BLM was developed in 2012 after the high-profile murder of Trayvon Martin, a teen who was returning home to a gated community in Florida after purchasing an Arizona Iced Tea and a bag of Skittles from a local convenience store when he was unlawfully profiled then gunned down by neighborhood watchman George Zimmerman, even though a local 911 operator instructed Zimmerman to leave

28. Ibid.
29. Black Lives Matter Movement, http://blacklivesmatter.com.

the teen boy alone. Zimmerman was acquitted of all charges, sparking national protest and unrest. The BLM movement's purpose is to create a self pride among African Americans and challenge other ethnicities to respect the dignity of African Americans. The organization seeks to institute legislation that protects and honors the self-worth of African Americans.

Our culture of violence has also been impacted by the development and selling of violence-ridden video games. According to Metacritic, the third-highest-rated video game of all time is "Grand Theft Auto IV" (2008) for the Playstation 3 game console.[30] The game has a concerning summary laced with celebrating unhealthy criminal behavior:

> What does the American Dream mean today? For Niko Belic, fresh off the boat from Europe. It's the hope he can escape his past. For his cousin, Roman, it is the vision that together they can find fortune in Liberty City, gateway to the land of opportunity. As they slip into debt and are dragged into a criminal underworld by a series of shysters, thieves and sociopaths, they discover that the reality is very different from the dream in a city that worships money and status, and is heaven for those who have them and a living nightmare for those who don't.[31]

"Grand Theft Auto IV" is rated M. According to the Entertainment Software Rating Board, a video game that's rated M means:

> Content is generally suitable for ages 17 and up. May contain intense violence, blood and gore, sexual content and/or strong language.[32]

The fact that any video game produced today has an M rating is alarming. The effects of youth and adults playing these games is damaging. According to the American Psychological Association,

---

30. "All Time Top-Rated Games," http://www.metacritic.com/browse/games/score/metascore/all/all/filtered.

31. Ibid.

32. ESRB Ratings Guide, https://www.esrb.org/ratings/ratings_guide.aspx.

"High levels of violent video game exposure have been linked to delinquency, fighting at school and during free play periods, and violent criminal behavior (e.g., self-reported assault, robbery)."[33] In addition to this, "meta-analyses reveal that violent video game effect sizes are larger than the effect of second hand tobacco smoke on lung cancer, the effect of lead exposure to I.Q. scores in children, and calcium intake on bone mass. Furthermore, the fact that so many youths are exposed to such high levels of video game violence further increases the societal costs of this risk factor."[34]

Last but not least, another contributing factor to our culture of violence is our Christian religion. Christianity is extremely violent. Sift through the Bible and you will find violent passages galore in both the Old and New Testament. Sometimes, it seems as if the "Good Book" really isn't that good. In my opinion, the most alarming text of terror featured in the Bible is the story of Hagar, a young servant girl of Abraham and Sarah who is forced to have sexual relations with Abraham, the "father of our faith," to bear a child for the inpatient couple who has struggled with infertility thus far. After Hagar conceives, Sarah becomes jealous and brutally beats Hagar then kicks her out of the couple's home. Hagar, who has been raped and beaten, is now homeless and pregnant. She escapes to the wilderness where she has an interesting encounter with God.

Hagar's story raises many parallels for us today in light of our culture of violence. First, Hagar is powerless compared to Abraham and Sarah. She's at Sarah and Abraham's beck and call. Hagar is treated like property or an object. Second, Hagar is the dirty little reminder that even those who are deemed in history to be our heroes, those we lift up as models to follow such as Abraham, may be anything but heroes. Hagar is the physical witness of Abraham's growing edges. Next, the exchange between Hagar and Sarah represents the dynamic that occurs when those who are all victims of the same oppressive system rage against each other instead of attacking the system that has placed the victims in this predicament. Also, Hagar's

33. Anderson, "Violent Video Games."
34. Ibid.

story reminds us of how people direct violence upon others who look like them and come from the same community as them. Last but not least, Hagar's story reminds us all of how we, at least once in our lifetime, have been in the wilderness. Hagar's story taps into our own feelings of alienation. We've all wrestled with feeling like it's us against the world. Worse yet, like Hagar, we've had to temporarily go back to places and spaces that have hurt us until our permanent liberation comes. As Phyllis Trible puts it:

> As a symbol of the oppressed, Hagar becomes many things to many people. Most specifically, all sorts of rejected women find their stories in her. She is the faithful maid exploited, the black woman used by the male and abused by the female of the ruling class, the surrogate mother, the resident alien without legal resource, the other woman, the runaway youth, the religious fleeing from affliction, the pregnant young woman alone, the expelled wife, the divorced mother with child, the shopping bag lady carrying bread and water, the homeless woman, the indigent relying upon handouts from the power structure, the welfare mother, and the self-effacing female whose own identity shrinks in service to others.[35]

How do you understand violence in our culture today? Better yet, how have you supported violence in our culture today? When was the last time you tuned in to your local box office and purchased tickets to the violence-ridden movies? When was the last time you bought the violence-ridden video games for your sons, daughters or grandchildren? How do you both support our government and hold our government accountable for our military beliefs and actions? Do you condone global violence or just peace? Do you stand in solidarity with #BlackLivesMatter, "Blue Lives Matter," or both? These are the questions me must struggle with in our quest to understand why gang violence permeates our society. Like it or not, these issues give birth to gangs and gang violence. Our challenge also lies in understanding how our sometimes ill-perceptions about gangs also contribute to the issue of gang violence.

35. Trible, *Texts of Terror*, 28.

III-Perceptions of How We Define "Gangs"

According to the National Gang Center, gangs are typically defined as follows:

- The group has three or more members, generally aged 12–24;
- Members share an identity, typically linked to a name, and often other symbols;
- Members view themselves as a gang, and they are recognized by others as a gang;
- The group has some permanence and a degree of organization;
- The group is involved in an elevated level of criminal activity.[36]

The center also explains:

> To remain in business, organized crime groups such as drug cartels must have strong leadership, codes of loyalty, severe sanctions for failure to abide by these codes, and a level of entrepreneurial expertise that enables them to accumulate and invest proceeds from drug sales. In contrast, "most street gangs are only loosely structured, with transient leadership and membership, easily transcended codes of loyalty, and informal rather than formal roles for the members." Very few street or youth gangs meet the essential criteria for classification as "organized crime."[37]

The challenge however with this definition causes concern. According to the National Gang Center, street gangs are defined differently from other types of gangs such as organized crime, ideology groups and hate groups made up of adult persons aged 25 and older. This is unfortunate because street gangs are primarily made up of poor persons of color, in particular underserved Hispanic/Latino and black/African Americans aged 12 to 24, while organized crime and hate group gangs are primarily made up of adult middle and upper-class white/European Americans.

36. Frequently Asked Questions about Gangs, https://www.nationalgangcenter.gov/About/FAQ#q1.

37. Ibid.

I believe this distinction is grounded in racism and classism and even ageism. By highlighting this distinction, the National Gang Center, a government-funded entity, draws a divide and thereby undergirds racial and socioeconomic stereotypes along with age discrimination. The definition of "gangs," as identified by the National Gang Center, creates a psychological perception that gangs are black and brown people, and thus elicits an emotional response when persons view and/or come in contact with black and brown youth.

I challenge our perception of how we define gangs. We primarily define a small number of people as a gang if they *primarily* participate in criminal activities. However, the National Institute of Justice says gangs' purpose is *in part* to engage in criminal activity:

> An association of three or more individuals; whose purpose in part is to engage in criminal activity and which uses violence or intimidation to further its criminal objectives.[38]

Thus, criminal activity is only one component of a gang's identity, but it is not the primary focus of the gang. Thus, I believe any social organization could be classified as a gang. It is the association of three or more individuals that is the primary identifying mark of a gang. I challenge us to think about other social organizations with three or more individuals as gangs too.

Unfortunately, we use the term "gang" as a negative connotation to describe street gangs, however other social organizations with three or more individuals are ascribed positive attributes. Why is this? Why don't we describe fraternities and sororities as gangs? Why don't we describe political affiliations as gangs? Why don't we define college affiliations as gangs? Maybe if we negate seeing street gangs as *only* participating in criminal activity, we can see the humanity in certain gang members. Maybe we won't label black and brown youth in definitive, deterministic terms. Maybe we can accord some grace and mercy to youth gangs as we seek to provide it's members with pastoral care and hopefully a new identity. Gangs

38. National Institute of Justice, "What Is a Gang?"

are not the problem. It's the criminal activity that is the problem. I compare gangs to guns. Guns don't kill people. People with guns kill other people. Thus, gangs do not hurt our society. It's the criminal behavior that some gang members *in part* participate in that hurts our society. After gaining some sense of social awareness about the patient, hospital chaplains make use of their time with gang member patients by engaging in the holy act of listening.

Listening as a Holy Act

What was most interesting about my encounter with Juan Carlos was the role listening played in his transformation. I am clear that there was nothing that I said to Juan Carlos during my initial visits that caused his new outlook on life. However, it was the listening ear that I provided him to express his feelings of alienation that surfaced from his inner core after reading the Isaiah passage in the Christ Hospital chapel. I then challenged his feelings of alienation by reminding him of his responsibility to be accountable to his older brother and the larger society by not participating in gang violence.

Listening is a holy act. According to Dr. Cari Jackson, "Holy activity is any action, or even thought intended to help people have greater awareness and experience of the divine life-giving power present in the universe."[39] Listening is a holy act because it allows individuals to experience the physical presence of God. Individuals experience the presence of God specifically through a hospital chaplain's listening ears. Most hospital patients view chaplains as symbolic representations of God, therefore, when a chaplain takes the time to listen to a patient, it is a holy act because the patient is left feeling valued, nurtured and loved by God. This is seen mainly in African spirituality: "Because spirituality in Africa is all-encompassing and inclusive, every human event, action, and interaction is sacred. This understanding makes every meeting and activity a sacred event," according to Dr. Lee Butler.[40]

39. Jackson, *Gift to Listen*, 3.
40. Butler, *Loving Home*, 51.

Listening is a very important skill to make use of in pastoral care and counseling. Jesus utilized this skill to connect with people. Even at 12 years of age, Jesus was mindful of the importance of listening.[41] He never grew out of the habit. Before ministering to needy people or telling them about the kingdom, he took the time to listen. He knew that to connect with people's hearts, he had to use his ears.

Listening is an important act. Families explode, marriages fall to pieces and relationships evaporate, when there is a lack of listening. Listening is a communal act which heals a broken community, according to Lee Butler.[42] This is because listening is synonymous with value. The value and worth of the speaker is dependent upon who listens, if any. Families erupt when relatives feel less than others because they have not been heard. Marriages fail when one spouse feels worthless because their counterpart doesn't heed their words. Relationships disintegrate when individuals feel slighted because second parties don't listen to them. Human beings' inability to maintain healthy relationships with each other will later cause an inability to maintain a healthy relationship with the Divine.[43]

Listening also fulfills human beings' universal need to be heard, according to Dr. Cari Jackson.[44] For example, when a little baby is born, he or she feels valued, loved and nurtured because they have the attention of their parents whenever they speak sounds or noises. As the baby grows and begins talking, the parents try to remain as attentive as possible to their baby's words. By doing this, the parents show the baby that they value his or her story. When the parents listen to the baby's story, they send a message that what the baby has to say is important, thus creating self-confidence and courage within the baby. When a baby speaks, if he or she is not given attention by their parents, the baby may grow into an adult who has low self-esteem and feels overlooked in society.

41. Luke 2:41–49.
42. Butler, *Loving Home*, 134.
43. 1 John 4:12.
44. Jackson, *Gift to Listen*, 10.

The Power of Story-Listening

Clergy also connect with gang members through the power of what Edward Wimberly calls "story-listening."[45] Story-listening is an important pastoral care strategy that demonstrates empathy. Story-listening, if done well, leaves one feeling cared for and loved first and foremost. The one sharing his or her story receives compassion, sensitivity and nonjudgment. In order for this to happen, it is important for the story-listener to refrain from giving quick clichés and scriptures and moving the person to immediately embrace hope. The story-listener must be willing to kick off their shoes, relax for a minute and wait, which is difficult in this microwave culture we live in today. The story-listener must be willing to sit in pain without immediately wanting to rush to joy.

Second, good story-listening asks the person sharing his or her story to reflect on when he or she was in a hopeless situation in the past before their current crisis. Reflection is pivotal in story-listening. Usually unfortunate transference and projection occur when the story-listener begins to insert their own experiences and beliefs in the pastoral encounter. The storyteller has to do the work for themselves and the story-listener must be quiet. The story-listener's job is to trigger or call into remembrance stories from the storyteller's past. The story-listener can do this by asking such reflective questions as:

My #
Res-
earch
Ques-
tions

- Tell me about a time when you were in a difficult situation?
- Tell me about a time when you felt like there was no solution in sight?
- Tell me about a time when you experienced a difficult dilemma that you thought was to hard for you to overcome?

Next, the story-listener challenges the storyteller to discuss the outcome of that past story and share how hope prevailed. Again, the story-listener must refrain from doing the work. It's up to the storyteller to reflect for him or herself. The story-listener then invites the storyteller to think about how their past story and current crisis is

45. Wimberly, *African American Pastoral Care*, 7–8.

similar. Hopefully, the story-listener will come to some conclusions that will give him or her encouragement in their current crisis. The person listening must be willing to accept that people can arrive at the destination without being given the answers. The listener must understand that people really do know the answers to their life problems, they simply need someone to bounce ideas off of.

Last but not least, the story-listener asks the storyteller to reflect on their own human agency from their past story and relate that to their human agency in their current crisis. The storyteller must remind the storyteller that they are gifted, skilled and talented and they have power in their situation no matter how chaotic it may be. The storyteller learns that they are not merely a passive entity or passerby in their own story, but a willing, active participant. Empowering persons in this process means people won't have to come back to us next time they find themselves in a fickle situation because they will start to work this process out for themselves. Regardless of where they are on their life's journey, when the next chaotic encounter occurs, they will remember the process of reflecting on a past experience and using past hope to propel them forward.

Working as story-listeners causes us to reflect on how we view and experience humanity in relationship to ourselves. Do we make space to hear others' stories? Do we allow people to share their open and honest feelings? Are people allowed to be totally vulnerable in our presence? Can we sit in pain without moving to "happy, happy, joy, joy"? Can we sit in despair without evangelizing, proselytizing or condemning what we believe is people's lack of faith? Can we honor the feelings and stories of others without making judgments, casting condemnation, or eliciting shame? Can we empower people to make their own life decisions or do we act like we know it all? Do we really believe people are smart enough to handle their own life crisis or do we see ourselves as little gods called to put on our capes and save the world? Do we create unhealthy relationships with people in which they need to always seek council from us like an addiction? Empathy means connecting with people in deeper, more meaningful ways that honor the living, breathing soul before us.

CHAPTER 4

Holding Accountability and Educating Gang Member Patients

AS A HISPANIC MALE struggling to survive in America with many obstacles facing him, Juan Carlos expresses feelings of alienation. To be honest, Juan Carlos is not affiliated with the Latin Kings gang because he can earn extra money, but because he feels alienated without any parental support and lonely without his older brother who is forced to work long hours. Ironically enough, I believe that the same feelings of alienation that Juan Carlos and other youth experience are shared by the children of Israel in Babylonian exile.

Both the experiences of youth in gangs and Israel in Babylon are similar. First, both groups experience disconnection from society. The children of Israel were deported to Babylon during their exilic periods, causing them to feel like outcasts while living in a different land. In 597 BC, under the direction of King Nebuchadnezzar, the Babylonian army partially destroyed the temple of Jerusalem and deported a large number of prominent Israeli citizens to Babylon. Eleven years later in 587/6 BC, under the reign of King Zedekiah, Babylon invaded Israel's land again and deported a second rising of influential individuals. In 581 BC, five years later, the Babylonians raided the children of Israel for a third time. As they had done twice before, the Babylonian army captured famous figures of Israel and brought them back to Babylon, as recorded in Jeremiah.

Youth in gangs also experience feelings of disconnection from society. Due to important sociological data already discussed, most youth who are affiliated with gangs are social outcasts. Usually, these individuals are delinquents in their community, having criminal records for drug-related crimes. Also, these individuals are outcasts in their schools, exhibiting poor academic records and high dropout rates.

Non-white youth in gangs also experience feelings of disconnection from society due to important historical data. Some youth have ancestors, who were deported against their will, to America from their native homelands. Unfortunately, some of these youth have never been able to break away from the psychological effects of their ancestors' illegal deportations. For example, many African American youth continue to live in mental and emotional bondage passed down from one generation to another since the period of African enslavement in America as was discussed.

In addition to both Israel in Babylon and youth in gangs experiencing feelings of disconnection from society, both groups experience the need to assimilate in order to survive. As I shared earlier, according to the University of Chicago's Center for the Study of Race, Politics and Culture, 45 percent of Hispanic youth believe "it's hard to get ahead because you face so much discrimination."[1] In fact, 30 percent of Hispanic youth think "you have to act white to get ahead."[2] In the case of Israel, unlike the Assyrians, who moved most of the people out and resettled the land with foreigners, King Nebuchadnezzar ordered only the strong and skilled leaders deported from Jerusalem, leaving the poor, uneducated and unskilled people to misrule and mislead what was left of Jerusalem.[3] The deported leaders, such as Daniel, were then forced to assimilate into a Babylonian culture quite different from their own; having even their birth

1. Cohen et al., "Attitudes and Behavior," 18.
2. Ibid.
3. 2 Kings 24:14.

names changed.[4] If these leaders chose to resist Nebuchadnezzar, they were gruesomely tortured and killed. Evidence of this can be seen in the story of Daniel's three friends (Shadrach, Meshach and Abednego) who were thrown into a fiery furnace after refusing to bow down and worship a statue of the king.[5]

Despite the feelings of alienation while in Babylonian exile, Israel chose to remain accountable to themselves and God. They remembered the promise of God spoken by the prophet Isaiah.[6] The children of Israel could have easily submerged themselves into the Babylonian culture, throwing away their understandings of God. Specifically, they could have easily done away with God's first commandment: "Thou shall have no other God before me,"[7] and worshipped the numerous false gods of the Babylonians. The children of Israel could have easily indulged in the food offered to the Babylonian gods also. However, Israel recognized that they must be faithful and loyal to their tradition. They had a responsibility to their families and loved ones who depended on them to carry on the traditions of their theology and culture. In other words, the children of Israel remembered that they were accountable to God and their community, therefore they must remain loyal to God and their community.

Accountability is a concept in ethics with several meanings. It is often used synonymously with such concepts as answerability, enforcement, responsibility, blameworthiness, liability and other terms associated with the expectation of account-giving. As an aspect of governance, it has been central to discussions related to problems in both the public and private (corporate) worlds. Accountability is defined as "A is accountable to B when A is obliged to inform B about A's (past or future) actions and decisions, to justify them, and to suffer punishment in the case of eventual misconduct."[8]

---

4. Daniel 1.
5. Daniel 3.
6. Isaiah 41:10.
7. Exodus 20:2.
8. Schedler, "Conceptualizing Accountability," 17.

Gang members must be told that they are accountable to God and to their community. God does not call human beings to commit acts of violence against each other ("Thou shall not kill"),[9] but God does call us to be accountable to one another. In the case of Juan Carlos, he realized that he was accountable to God and his brother, therefore he could not continue down a path of destruction by participating in violent behavior. In some sense, I invited Juan Carlos to embrace a differentiation of self or new identity apart from his gang "family."

Self-Differentiation from the Gang Family

It is possible to leave a gang. Most times, gang members leave a gang by "retiring."[10] There are three primary ways that gang members retire:

- Physically moving to a different neighborhood;
- Gaining employment, beginning a new career path, going back to school for further/higher education;
- Settling down and starting a family/marrying and having children.

The term *self-differentiate* is highlighted in family systems theory, which asserts that we are who we are based on influential messages that have been passed on to us by influential family members.[11] These messages have a tendency to either help us or hinder us in our adulthood. These messages help us realize our full potential or hinder us from living our authentic mission and purpose. Thus, the purpose of life is for one to develop their own unique identity by both incorporating helpful messages from the past and leaving behind unhelpful messages from the past.

The gang functions like a family. In the gang family, there are messages that have been imbedded in the psyche of the members.

9. Exodus 20:12.

10. Walden, "Ex-Gang Member."

11. Boyd-Franklin, *Black Families in Therapy*, 126.

Some of those messages may be helpful. For example, many gangs instill in their members a sense of pride and confidence. Pride and confidence are wonderful attributes that a gang member can hold onto throughout the rest of their life's journey. On the other hand, many gangs also instill in their members behaviors of fear, control, and dominance. These behaviors are not helpful for a gang member to hold onto for the rest of their life's journey.

In pastoral care encounters, I invite clergy to help gang members self-differentiate or create a new identity apart from the gang. This occurs through the process of asking reflective questioning such as:

- What are your gifts and skills (outside of the gang)?
- What do you like to do for fun?
- What do you think you do well?
- What are your hopes and dreams?
- What needs to happen for you to accomplish your hopes and dreams?
- What are your aspirations?
- What needs to happen for you to accomplish your aspirations?
- What are the benefits to being a part of your gang?
- What are the consequences to being a part of your gang?
- What does your gang do well?
- What does your gang do not so well?

Reflecting on these questions helps gang members start to grapple with a new identity. Also, reflecting on these questions helps gang members think out loud about specific strategies and interventions to develop their new identity.

It's important to note that breaking away totally from a gang is very, very difficult. Similarly, leaving one's family is very difficult. So I challenge clergy to exercise patience and sensitivity to gang members seeking to develop new identities. Our lives are like airplanes and airplane runways. All of us have airplanes and all of us have runways. Some of us have short runways because our planes leave the ground quicker while others may have longer runways because it may take their plane longer to take off. No runway is better than another. The purpose of life, no matter how long it takes, is simply to learn to take off. No passenger on an airplane ever rates the distance of the runway. The only thing the passenger cares about is getting to their final destination safe and sound. Such is life. As long as gang members arrive safe and sound to their final destination, which is a life of healing, hope and wholeness, that's all that counts.

CHAPTER 5

Ending on Empowerment

LAST BUT NOT LEAST, gang members need empowerment from chaplains and community clergy. Empowerment means understanding that everyone, regardless of race, ethnicity, nationality, gender, sexual orientation, age, or social status, has gifts and skills that have been implanted in them from the Divine. Everyone was born into the world with unique talents that shape their identity and foster their mission and purpose in life. Sometimes, persons have a hard time discerning their gifts, skills and talents. Reflective processes such as therapy or clinical pastoral education invite persons to reflect on their strengths. Chaplains and community clergy can act as mirrors to help people see their gifts.

Unfortunately, some people have trouble seeing their gifts even if they have the mirror of a certified therapist and/or CPE supervisor and church pastor. Nancy Boyd-Franklin asserts that victims of oppression wrestle with identifying and even believing in their strengths.[1] Persons of oppression wrestle with gaining their confidence and walking in their authentic, genuine self. Boyd-Franklin says that there are certain people who struggle with seeing their gifts, particularly if they are a person of color and living in a lower economic bracket.[2] Specifically, Boyd-Franklin points to poor African Americans who struggle the most with seeing their gifts:

1. Boyd-Franklin, *Black Families in Therapy*, 166.
2. Ibid.

Unlike other cultural or ethnic groups who can "blend in" or become part of the "melting pot," Black people by virtue of skin color are visible reminders of the inequities of society. With this experience of victimization comes a sense of powerlessness and, for many Black families, a sense of entrapment. This sense of being unable to make and implement basic life decisions in their own lives and the lives of their children often leads to a sense of futility. Empowerment most often involves helping parents to regain control of their families and feel that they can effect important changes for themselves.[3]

How do we empower persons of victimization? One way is to ask persons to think and talk out loud about their own gifts, skills and talents:

- What do you have going for yourself?
- What are your passions?
- What do you do well?
- What gives you life?

Another gift that persons of victimization have that's often overlooked is the ability to be resourceful in the midst of having no resources. When my mother and father struggled to provide food for my brothers and me during tough economic times, I was always amazed at a simple, yet very resourceful act that my mother would organize. She would gather what she did have, such as two pounds of ground beef, and she would knock on our next door neighbors' homes, one by one, and ask them to add an ingredient to her ground beef. By the time she was done, we ate a huge stew filled with not only beef but corn, noodles, green beans, tomato sauce and okra. And everybody would eat until they were stuffed! That's what it means to be resourceful. To make a way out of no way. To assess a situation and provide crisis management. To triage an issue currently on life support.

3. Ibid., 279.

CHAPTER 6

What about Me?

Self-Care for the Pastoral Care Provider to Practice

IT'S 8:00 A.M. I can still see the sun rising. I slowly pull up in front of my apartment. I can barely parallel park my car. I'm soooooo tired. A family emergency happened to the chaplain who was suppose to relieve me at 11:30 p.m. so I ended up working a double shift. And I'm paying for it now. I slowly shift my weight and hobble out of my car, regretting that I didn't buy a truck last year instead. I decide I'm not gonna lug my bags out, I'll be returning to work in a little while so there's no point. I simply make sure my car doors are locked and I stumble to my front door. I feel like I'm drunk.

"Late night partying again, Rev?"

I look at my next door neighbor. I make a sarcastic facial gesture. He starts to laugh.

"Just kidding, get some rest today Rev, before you have to go back out with the animals again tonight. It's a jungle out there!"

"You're telling me, Sam. Good night."

I stumble into the main foyer of the apartment complex. I don't even bother to see if I have any mail. I look up at the long winding stairs before me. Damn! Why did I move onto the third floor! Well, no use in going slow. I muster up enough energy to run up the stairs with my last, and I mean my last, little bit of energy. I grab my house keys from my pocket and realize that I've disturbed my bowels with running up the stairs. I gotta pee now! I quickly jiggle my keys in the door lock and like a tornado I slam the door open and race to the bathroom. I drop my pants just in time. Exhale!

Attending to my own physical, emotional and spiritual well-being is very important in my pastoral care work. Practicing self-care prevents burnout, which is a state of physical, emotional, and mental exhaustion caused by involvement in situations that are emotionally demanding, accompanied by disillusionment and negative feelings. Signs of burnout include fatigue, irritability, somatic complaints, feeling that life is less fun, decreased empathy, and reduced sense of accomplishment. Burnout usually begins gradually, and over time takes a toll on the psyche and physical health. There are several types of burnouts that can be experienced. "Compassion Fatigue,"[1] a phrase coined by Charles Figley, is a type of burnout that comes from exposure to people's suffering, particularly those exposed to traumatic events. This is secondary stress.

There are several strategies I incorporate in my commitment to self-care to avoid burnout and specifically "compassion fatigue." I believe there is a connection between mind, body and spirit. When I am ailing in any one of these three areas, it indirectly affects the other two areas. For example, when I am worried about an issue, I usually experience body aches and pains. At the same time, when I am joyous and hopeful, then I usually experience a desire to be physically active. Therefore, I participate in self-care activities that address each of the three parts of my being—my physical, emotional and spiritual aspects of self.

Physical Self-Care

I engage in several activities to strengthen my emotional and spiritual well-being. I have observed that certain physical activities affect my emotional being or mood. The following is a list of physical activities that I do to help me maintain a pleasant mood:

---

1. "Did You Know?," http://www.compassionfatigue.org.

- Exercising (swimming, basketball, running, etc.)
- Quilting, knitting, crocheting
- Journaling/writing in a diary
- Eating a healthy, delicious meal
- People watching / meeting someone new
- Walking through a park / observing nature
- Adopting/playing with a pet animal
- Taking a warm bath/shower
- Meditation/yoga
- Listening to peaceful music
- Traveling
- Taking time off from work from time to time
- Watching a peaceful, violence-free movie
- Coloring, drawing, arts
- Attending a spa

Emotional Self-Care

I do several activities to increase my emotional well-being. First, I try to think helpful thoughts and refrain from thinking unhelpful thoughts. Here are methods I practice to decrease unhelpful thoughts:

- Stopping unhealthy thoughts when I realizing they are occurring, changing my thoughts to positive feelings or events.

- Worrying about an issue for only a small amount of time then focusing my attention on something else that will captivate my mind.

- Imagining the worst that could happen in a situation then reflecting on how my current situation is not that bad.

- Gaining serenity and peace (if I can't change it, I'll join it).[2]

My emotional health is also dependent upon limiting or ending my cognitive distortions. There are ten types of cognitive distortions:

1. All or nothing thinking: Viewing things in black and white categories. If my performance falls short of "perfect," I see myself as a total failure.

2. Overgeneralization: Viewing a single negative event as a never-ending pattern of defeat.

3. Mental filter: I pick out a single negative detail and dwell on it exclusively so that my vision of all reality becomes darkened.

4. Disqualifying the positive: I reject positive experiences by insisting they "don't count" for some reason, therefore I can maintain a negative belief that is contradicted by everyday experiences.

5. Jumping to conclusions: I make a negative interpretation by trying to mind read or anticipate the future even though there are no definite facts that accurately support my conclusion.

6. Magnification or minimization: I exaggerate the importance of things (such as my mistakes or someone else's achievements), or I inappropriately shrink things until they appear tiny (my own desirable qualities or someone else's imperfections).

7. Emotional reasoning: I assume that my negative emotions necessarily reflect the way things function. In other words, "I feel it, therefore it must be true."

8. "Should" and "Must" statements: I place pressure and stress on myself to accomplish certain tasks. For example, "I must graduate from school this year or I will be a failure." If I am unable to accomplish these tasks, I place blame and guilt on myself. For example, "I should not have married my ex-spouse, then I would not be struggling with this divorce process."

2. See GPA South Gippsland's "Self Care Strategies" workbook.

9. Labeling and mislabeling: This is an extreme form or over-generalization. Instead of describing my error, I attach a negative label to myself: "I'm a loser." When someone else's behavior rubs me the wrong way, I attach a negative label to the person. For example, "He's a pain in the neck." Mislabeling involves describing an event with language that is highly colored and emotionally loaded.

10. Personalization: I see myself as the cause of some negative external event, which in fact I was not primarily responsible for.[3]

Spiritual Self-Care

Several Bible passages promote spiritual self-care.

- Philippians 2:4 (NIV): "Each of you should look not only to your own interests, but also to the interests of others."

- Galatians 6:2–5 (NIV): "Carry each other's burdens, and in this way you will fulfill the law of Christ. If anyone thinks he is something when he is nothing, he deceives himself. Each one should test his own actions. Then he can take pride in himself, without comparing himself to somebody else, for each one should carry his own load."

- Luke 2:49 (NIV): "Didn't you know I needed to be in my Father's house?"

- Luke 5:15–16 (NIV): "Yet the news about him spread all the more, so that crowds of people came to hear him and to be healed of their sicknesses. But Jesus often withdrew to lonely places and prayed."

- Mark 1:35–38 (NIV): "Very early in the morning, while it was still dark, Jesus got up, left the house and went off to a solitary place where he prayed. . . . Disciples went to look for him . . . they exclaimed, 'Everyone is looking for you!'"

3. Ibid.

I nurture myself spiritually through:

- Prayer
- Meditation
- Reading and reflecting on devotional materials
- Singing hymns / listening to gospel music
- Attending worship services (that I am *not* facilitating or participating in)
- Listening to phenomenal preaching
- Reading and reflecting on Bible passages

When was the last time you participated in a self-care activity? It's so important to resist what I call the "spirit of busy." The spirit of busy is what Martha struggled with in Luke 10:38–42. Martha was so busy tending to the household needs, that she couldn't sit and be content in the presence of Jesus. Busyness is seductive. We live in a society where we qualify our worth based on the quantity of our work. I believe this stems from our lack of self-confidence. We don't trust ourselves. We don't trust in our identities. We don't trust in our gifts and skills. So we overcompensate by working long, excruciating years, months, days and hours to prove ourselves. Prove we are called to do this. Prove that we have the capabilities to this. When we finally reach a place of confidence, we will be good to ourselves—our minds, bodies and spirits. Being good to ourselves will cause a chain reaction whereby we will be good to others as well. As the saying goes, "hurt people, hurt people." Self-care is a quest to love ourselves so we, in turn, can love other people. The question to grapple with is "Do you love yourself?" Today is a new day to start.

CHAPTER 7

Where Do We Go from Here?

I RECENTLY FLEW TO New Orleans to guest preach at St. John's Faith #5 at the invitation of a close friend, Antoine Mason. I had never been to the French Quarter before, neither had I visited Bourbon Street. I decided to venture out and see what new experiences awaited me. As I walked down Bourben Street I took in all the sights and sounds of my wildest imagination. Suddenly a beautiful sista' with a deep New Orleans accent jumped in front of my path and asked me if I wanted to take a shot of rum and other "special flavors" with her. Hey, I was up for the challenge. You only live once according to Aubrey Graham so I prepared my palate for what I was getting ready to take in. To my surprise, she poured her special concoction into two small test tube-looking contraptions then proceeded to place the bottom end of the filled tubes in her mouth. Without any hesitation she then invited me to open my mouth at which point she'd pour the alcohol from the top open end into my mouth. That's when I copped out like a chicken. I quickly assessed that our mouths would eventually meet if I participated in this endeavor. I quickly backed up and walked away. She started screaming expletives at me as I walked away. I was so embarrassed as others along Bourbon began staring at me and looking back at her. I tried to keep walking through the bustle of people crowded along the street.

Suddenly, something magical if not spiritual happened. My traveling companion whispered, "That's Trayvon Martin's mother. . . ." I turned to see a stoic, classy beautiful woman standing alongside Bourbon Street gazing at the spectacle. I mustered up enough courage to ask, "Are you Trayvon Martin's mother?" At first she looked surprised and said, "No. . . ." Then I noticed her traveling companions drop their heads and smile. I gazed back at her and a small smile creeped from the corner of her mouth. I smiled back. "Yes," she said. "I'm Trayvon's mother."

Then it happened. I froze. I became sad, mad, scared all in one. Here, standing in front of me, was Sybrina Fulton. I remembered her face, her hairstyle, even her lipstick from countless television news stories, newspaper articles and magazine features. I froze. A lump formed in my throat. She looked at me with a tiredness in her eyes. She looked peaceful, yet still hurt from justice unserved. For those brief seconds as I searched for something, anything to say, visions of Emmett Till flooded my mind. I psychologically checked out as my mind wandered to the cotton fields of Georgia. I imagined my ancestors' blood on those cotton fields. Then my mind fast-forwarded to the bus boycotts of Montgomery, Alabama. I thought about young polite negroes sitting at lunch counters being spat on, punched and kicked by racist white folk. I imagined young black college students bearing the stinging pain of water hoses and dog bites. My mind raced to Sybrina Fulton's son, Trayvon. I imagined him walking home with his Arizona Iced Tea and bag of Skittles before coming face to face with George Zimmerman. Then my mind raced to Tamir Rice, Sandra Bland, Freddie Gray, Alton Sterling and most recently this year, Terence Crutcher. God damn. I fought the urge to cry. I fought the urge to scream. I fought the urge to kick any and every white person's ass I saw for the rest of the day. I simply gave Sybrina Fulton a hug, told her I was praying for her and slowly walked away.

Where do we go from here? When I think about gang violence I become enraged. We are dying in so many other forms and fashions, gang violence becomes another lethal weapon. But my rage is not what's needed in these moments. Temporary anger is meaningless if not connected to long-term action. Where do we go from here? It's time to act. Where do we go from here?

One word: talking. It's time to start talking, having authentic genuine conversations. Not becoming choked up like I was standing in front of Sybrina Fulton. Be unafraid to go there. Having the tough conversations. Talking about why gang violence is so prevalent in our communities today. Not blaming societal ills, not blaming parents, not shaming gang members but openly dialoguing about the needs of our most vulnerable who feel as if gang violence is the answer. Where's their voice? Are we giving them space to share? Or are the voices of the social elite crowding our space?

We must do more than talk to each other. We must talk to gang members. Get inside their world. Find out their hopes, passions and dreams. Engage the powers. We must discover what makes them tick. We must ask them what they need from us. We must stop prescribing what we think they need. We must stop assuming that we have the answers.

Then and only then will we be able to tackle *our* gang violence problem. This impacts all of us. Whether you live in middle-class white suburbia or the inner city. Gang violence connects us all. The threads of violence are far reaching. Like a spider web we are all entangled.

Where do we go from here? To the gangs in our communities. We create space to talk to them. When is the last time you engaged the gang members in your own neighborhood? Don't pretend they don't exist. Don't pretend they are not there. They are. And they are waiting on you. Can you finally step out to them? Who are the high-ranking gang members in your area? What are their names? Who are upper-level ones who manage the lower-level members? Where do they reside? When was the last time you interacted with them? When was the last time you invited them to your house for dinner? Made them feel comfortable? If you can't answer these questions with any relevancy, there just may be a deeper issue than simply gang violence. . . .

Bibliography

Anderson, Craig A. "Violent Video Games: Myths, Facts, and Unanswered Questions." APA, Science Briefs, October 2003. http://www.apa.org/science/about/psa/2003/10/anderson.aspx.

Anderson, Craig A., et al. "Exposure to Violent Media: The Effects of Songs with Violent Lyrics on Aggressive Thoughts and Feelings." *Journal of Personality and Social Psychology* 84 (2003) 960–71. http://www.apa.org/pubs/journals/releases/psp-845960.pdf.

Boyd-Franklin, Nancy. *Black Families in Therapy: A Multisystems Approach.* New York: Guilford, 1989.

Butler, Lee. *A Loving Home: Caring for African American Marriage and Families.* Cleveland: Pilgrim, 2000.

Cohen, Cathy J., et al. "The Attitudes and Behavior of Young Black Americans: Research Summary." University of Chicago Center for the Study of Race, Politics, and Culture, February 2007. http://www-news.uchicago.edu/releases/07/070201.blackyouthproject.pdf.

Crigger, Megan, and Laura Santhanam. "How Many Americans Have Died in U.S. Wars?" PBS.org, May 24, 2015. http://www.pbs.org/newshour/updates/many-americans-died-u-s-wars.

Douglas, Kelly Brown. *The Black Christ.* Maryknoll: Orbis, 1994.

Egley, Arlen, Jr., et al. "Highlights of the 2012 National Youth Gang Survey." US Dept. of Justice, December 2014. http://www.ojjdp.gov/pubs/248025.pdf.

General Practice Alliance [GPA] South Gippsland. "Self Care Strategies: A Workbook to Help Promote Emotional Wellbeing." http://www.actassupport.com.au/pdf/gpa_self_care_strategies_workbook.pdf.

Jackson, Cari. *The Gift to Listen: The Courage to Hear.* Minneapolis: Augsburg Fortress, 2003.

Linker, Damon. "Why America Can't Break Out of the Cycle of Never-Ending War." *The Week*, September 24, 2014. http://theweek.com/articles/443537/why-america-cant-break-cycle-neverending-war.

McCann, Mac. "The 30 Most Disturbing Songs of All Time." *Dallas Observer*, August 19, 2013. http://www.dallasobserver.com/music/the-30-most-disturbing-songs-of-all-time-7057625.

Richardson, Ronald. *Creating a Healthier Church: Family Systems Theory, Leadership and Congregational Life*. Minneapolis: Augsburg Fortress, 1996.

Schedler, Andreas. "Conceptualizing Accountability." In *The Self-Restraining State: Power and Accountability in New Democracies*, edited by Schedler et al., 13–28. Boulder, CO: Rienner, 1999. Available online at http://www.follesdal.net/projects/ratify/TXT/Paris_Schedler.PDF.

Trible, Phyllis. *Texts of Terror: Literary-Feminist Readings of Biblical Narratives*. Minneapolis: Augsburg Fortress, 1984.

Valdemar, Richard. "Skinhead and Other White Supremacist Gangs: Understanding the Markings and Motivations of White Supremacist Gangs." *Police* (magazine), July 13, 2007. http://www.policemag.com/blog/gangs/story/2007/07/skinhead-and-other-white-supremacist-gangs.aspx.

Walden, Tiffany. "Ex-Gang Member Says It Is Possible to Retire from Gang Life." *Medill Reports* (Northwestern University), February 22, 2012. http://newsarchive.medill.northwestern.edu/chicago/news-200885.html.

Wimberly, Edward. *African American Pastoral Care*. Nashville: Abingdon, 2008.